was passionate, explosive, and utterly wonderful *Part of That World*

'J. Kenner's evocative writing thrillingly captures the power of physical attraction, the pull of longing, the universe-altering effect one person can have on another. She masterfully draws out the eroticism between Nikki and Damien . . . *Claim Me* has the emotional depth to back up the sex . . . Every scene is infused with both erotic tension, and the tension of wor   how and when it wi

'*Claim Me* by J. Kenner is an erotic, sexy and exciting ride. The story between Damien and Nikki is amazing and written beautifully. The intimate and detailed sex scenes will leave you fanning yourself to cool down. With the writing style of Ms Kenner you almost feel like you are there in the story riding along the emotional rollercoaster with Damien and Nikki' *Fresh Fiction*

'PERFECT for fans of *Fifty Shades of Grey* and *Bared to You*. *Release Me* is a powerful and erotic romance novel that is sure to make adult romance readers sweat, sigh and swoon' *Reading, Eating & Dreaming Blog*

'*Release Me* . . . just made the top of my list with Damien and Nikki . . . the way in which J. Kenner tells the story, how vulnerable and real Damien and Nikki feel, makes this story so good, and re-readable many times over' *In Love With Romance Blog*

'This is deeply sensual and the story packs an emotional punch that I really hadn't expected . . . If you enjoyed *Fifty Shades* [and] the Crossfire books, you're definitely going to enjoy this one. It's compelling, engaging and I was thoroughly engrossed' *Sinfully Sexy Blog*

'I will admit, I am in the "I loved *Fifty Shades*" camp, but after reading *Release Me*, Mr Grey only scratches the surface compared to Damien Stark' *Cocktails and Books Blog*

'It is not often when a book is so amazingly well-written that I find it hard to even begin to accurately describe it . . . I recommend this book to everyone who is interested in a passionate love story' *Romancebookworm's Reviews*

'The story is one that will rank up with the *Fifty Shades* and Crossfire trilogies' *Incubus Publishing Blog*

'*Release Me* gives readers tantalizing pages of sensual delight, leaving us reeling as we journey with this couple and their passions are released. *Release Me* is a must-read!' *Readaholics Anonymous*

J. Kenner (aka Julie Kenner) is the *New York Times, USA Today, Publishers Weekly, Wall Street Journal*, and No. 1 internationally bestselling author of over seventy novels, novellas, and short stories in a variety of genres.

Though known primarily for her award-winning and internationally bestselling erotic romances (including the Stark and Most Wanted series) that have reached as high as No. 2 on the *New York Times* bestseller list, Kenner has been writing full-time for over a decade in a variety of genres, including paranormal and contemporary romance, 'chicklit' suspense, urban fantasy, and paranormal mommy lit.

Kenner has been praised by *Publishers Weekly* as an author with a 'flair for dialogue and eccentric characterizations' and by *Romantic Times* for having 'cornered the market on sinfully attractive, dominant antiheroes and the women who swoon for them'. A five-time finalist for Romance Writers of America's prestigious RITA award, Kenner took home the first RITA trophy awarded in the category of erotic romance in 2014 for her novel *Claim Me* (book two of her Stark Trilogy). Her books have sold well over a million copies and are published in over twenty countries.

In her previous career as an attorney, Kenner worked as a lawyer in Southern California and Texas. She currently lives in Central Texas with her husband, two daughters and two cats.

Visit J. Kenner online at **www.jkenner.com**. Or connect with her via Twitter **@juliekenner** or through **www.facebook.com/JKennerBooks**.

By J. Kenner

The Stark Series
Release Me
Claim Me
Complete Me
Anchor Me

The Stark Ever After Novellas
Take Me (e-novella)
Have Me (e-novella)
Play My Game (e-novella)
Seduce Me (e-novella)
Unwrap Me (e-novella)
Deepest Kiss (e-novella)
Entice Me (e-novella)

The Stark International Series
Say My Name
On My Knees
Under My Skin
Steal My Heart (free short story)
Take My Dare (e-novella)

The S.I.N. Series
Dirtiest Secret
Hottest Mess
Sweetest Taboo

The Most Wanted Series
Wanted
Heated
Ignited

JKENNER

ANCHOR Me

HEADLINE
ETERNAL

First published in Great Britain in 2017
by HEADLINE ETERNAL
An imprint of HEADLINE PUBLISHING GROUP

1

Cataloguing in Publication Data is available from the British Library

ISBN 978 1 4722 4686 8

Typeset in 11/14 pt Minion Pro by Jouve (UK), Milton Keynes

Printed and bound in Great Britain by CPI Group (UK) Ltd, Croydon, CR0 4YY

HEADLINE PUBLISHING GROUP
An Hachette UK Company
Carmelite House
50 Victoria Embankment
London EC4Y 0DZ

www.headlineeternal.com
www.headline.co.uk
www.hachette.co.uk

For Isabella, with love.

I

I look out the window at the beautifully manicured yards that line the wide street down which I am traveling in the sumptuous luxury of a classic Rolls Royce Phantom. A car so sleek and magical that I can't help but feel like a princess in a royal coach.

The road is shaded by parallel rows of massive oaks, their branches arcing over the street toward their counterparts to form a leafy canopy. Morning light fights its way between the leaves, creating golden beams in which dust sparkles and dances as if to a celebratory melody, adding to the illusion that we are moving through a fairy tale world.

All in all, it's a picture-perfect moment.

Except it's not. Not really. Or at least not to me.

Because as far as I'm concerned, this is no children's story.

This is Dallas. This is the neighborhood where I grew up. And that means that this isn't a fairy tale. It's a nightmare.

The branches aren't stunning—they're grasping. Reaching out to snare me. To hold me tight. To trap me.

The canopy doesn't mark a royal corridor leading to a castle. It leads to a cell. And it's not *The Dance of the Sugarplum Fairies* that fills the air. It is a requiem for the dead.

The world outside the car is lined with traps, and if I'm not careful, I'll be sucked in. Destroyed by the darkness that hides behind the false facades of these stately houses. Surrounded not by a bright children's tale, but by a horror movie, lured in by the promise of beauty and then trapped forever and slowly destroyed, ripped to pieces by the monsters in the dark.

Breathe, I tell myself. *You can do this. You just have to remember to breathe.*

"Nikki. *Nikki.*"

Damien's voice startles me back to reality, and I jerk upright, calling upon perfect posture to ward off the ghosts of my memories.

His tone is soft, profoundly gentle, but when I glance toward him, I see that his eyes have dipped to my lap.

For a moment, I'm confused, then I realize that I've inched up my skirt, and my fingertip is slowly tracing the violent scar that mars my inner thigh. A souvenir of the deep, ugly wound that I inflicted upon myself a decade ago when I was desperate to find a way to release all the pent-up anger and fear and pain that swirled inside me like a phalanx of demons.

I yank my hand away, then turn to look out the window, feeling oddly, stupidly ashamed.

He says nothing, but the car moves to the curb and then rolls to a stop. A moment later, Damien's fingers twine with mine. I hold tight, drawing strength, and when I shift to look at him more directly, I see worry etched in the hard angles of that perfect face and reflected in those exceptional, dual-colored eyes.

Worry, yes. But it is the rest of what I see that takes my breath away. Understanding. Support. Respect.

Most of all, I see a love so fierce it has the power to melt me, and I revel in its power to soothe.

He is the biggest miracle of my life, and there are moments when I still can't believe that he is mine.

Damien Stark. My husband, my lover, my best friend. A man who commands an empire with a firm, controlling hand. Who takes orders from no one, and yet today is playing chauffeur so that he can stand beside me while I confront my past.

For a moment, I simply soak him in. His strength, apparent in both his commanding manner and the long, lean lines of his athletic body. His support reflected in those eyes that see me so intimately. That have, over the years, learned all my secrets.

Damien knows every scar on my body, as well as the story behind each. He knows the depth of my pain, and he knows how far I have come. How far his love has helped me come.

Most of all, he knows what it has cost me to return to Texas. To drive these streets. To look out at this neighborhood so full of pain and dark memories.

With a small shiver, I pull my hand free so that I can hug myself.

"Oh, baby." The concern in his voice is so thick I can almost grab hold of it. "Nikki, you don't have to do this."

"I do." My words sound ragged, my throat too clogged with unshed tears to speak normally.

"Sweetheart—"

I wait, expecting him to continue, but he's gone silent. I see the tension on his face, as if he's uncertain what to say or how to say it—but Damien Stark is never unsure. Not about business. Not about himself. Not about me.

And yet right now he's hesitating. Treating me like I'm something fragile and breakable.

An unexpected shock of anger cuts through me. Not at him, but at myself. Because, dammit, he's right. In this moment, I'm as fragile as I've ever been, and that's not a pleasant realization. I've fought so hard to be strong, and with Damien at my side, I've succeeded.

But here I am, all my hard work shot to hell simply because I've returned to my hometown.

"You think coming here is a mistake." I snap the words at him, but it's not Damien I'm irritated with, it's me.

"No." He doesn't hesitate, and I take some comfort in the speed and certainty of his response. "But I do wonder if now is the right time. Maybe tomorrow would be better. After your meetings."

We've come to Texas not so that I can torture myself by driving through my old neighborhood to visit my estranged mother, but because I'm vying to land a contract with one of the top web development companies in the country. It's looking to roll out a series of apps, both for internal use among its employees and externally for its clients.

I'd submitted a proposal and am now one of only five companies invited to come to Dallas to pitch, and my little company is by far the smallest and the newest. I suspect, of course, that part of the reason I got the invitation is because I'm married to Damien Stark, and because my company has already licensed software to Stark International.

A year ago, that would have bothered me.

Not anymore. I'm damn good at what I do, and if my last name gets me a foot in the door, then so be it. I don't care how the opportunity comes because I know that my work is top-notch, and if I get the job, it will be on the merits of my proposal and my presentation.

It's a huge opportunity, and one I don't want to screw up. Especially since my goal for the next eighteen months is to build up my receivables, hire five employees, and take over the full floor of the building that houses my office condo.

I'd worked on my business plan for months, and was a complete nervous wreck the night I handed it to my master of the universe, brilliantly entrepreneurial husband for review. When he'd given it the Damien Stark seal of approval, I practically collapsed with relief. My plan to grow my business doesn't hinge on me getting this job—but landing it will mean I can bump all my target dates up by six months. More importantly, winning this contract will put my business firmly on the competitive map.

My shoulders sag a bit as I meet his eyes. "You're afraid that seeing Mother is going to throw me off my game. That I'll flub tomorrow's meetings and hurt my chances of landing the contract."

"I want you at your best."

"I know you do," I say sincerely, because Damien has never been anything but supportive. "Don't you get it? That's why we're here. It's like a preemptive strike."

His brow furrows, but before he can ask what I mean, I rush to explain. "Just being in Dallas messes with my head—we both know that. She haunts this town. And having you here with me now makes it so much better. But you can't always be with me, and before I make my pitch, I need to be certain that I can travel back and forth between LA and Dallas without being afraid I'll see her around every corner."

The pathetic truth is that lately I've been seeing my mother around all sorts of corners. I've imagined seeing her in Beverly Hills shopping centers. On Malibu beaches. In crowded streets. At charity events. I have no idea why this woman I've worked so hard to block from my mind is suddenly at the forefront of my imagination, but she is.

And I really don't want her there.

I draw a breath, hoping he understands. "I need to lay all these demons to rest and just do my work. Please," I add, my voice imploring. "Please tell me you understand."

"I do," he says, then takes my hand and gently kisses my fingertips. As he does, his phone rings. It's sitting on the console, and I can see that the caller is his attorney, Charles Maynard.

"Don't you need to take it?" I ask, as he scowls, then declines the call.

"It can wait."

There's a hard edge to his voice, and I wonder what he's not telling me. Not that Damien keeps me informed about every aspect of his business—considering he pretty much owns and operates the entire planet and a few distant solar systems, that would require far too many updates—but he does tend to keep me in the loop on things that are troubling him.

I frown. It's clear that he's not telling me because I already have plenty on my mind. And while I appreciate the sentiment, I don't like that—once again—my mother has come between my husband and me.

"You should call him back," I say. "If he's calling on a Sunday, it must be important . . ."

I let the words trail away, hoping to give him an opening, but all he does is shake his head. "Don't worry about it," he says, even as his phone signals an incoming text.

He snatches it up, but not before I see Charles's name flash on the lock screen again, this time with a single word: *Urgent.*

Damien meets my eyes, and for just a moment his frustration is almost comical. Then he snatches up the phone and hits the button to call Charles. A second later, he's saying, "Dammit, I told you I can't be bothered with this right now."

He listens to the response, the furrows in his brow growing deeper. Finally, he sighs, looking more frustrated than I've seen him in a long time.

Cold foreboding washes over me. Damien isn't the kind of man who gets frustrated over business deals. On the contrary, the harder and more challenging the deal, the more he thrives.

Which means this is personal.

"I hear you, Charles, but I'm not paying you for your advice on this. I'm paying you for those resources you're so keen on touting. So use them, dammit. Pull out all the stops and get me some answers by the time I'm back in LA. Fine," he adds after another pause. "Call me if you have something definitive. Otherwise I'll see you in a couple of days."

He ends the call and slams the phone back down. I open my mouth, intending to ask him what's happening, but before I get the chance, he pulls me roughly to him and closes his mouth over mine. The kiss is hard, brutal, and I slide closer, losing myself in the wildness. And for this moment at least, I forget my apprehension and his problems. There is nothing but us, our passion a raging blaze that clears away the debris of our lives, stripping us to the bone until there is nothing left but the two of us.

I'm breathing hard when we break apart, my lips bruised and tingling, my body burning. I want to turn around and go back to the hotel. I want to strip off my clothes and feel his hands on me, his cock inside me. I want it wild. Raw. Pain and pleasure so intense I get lost in them. Passion so violent it breaks me. And Damien—always Damien—right there to put me back together again.

I want, but I can't have. Not yet. Because whatever else is going on, I've come to this neighborhood with a purpose, and if I back away now, I may not have the strength to return.

And so, as Damien holds me close, I press my cheek against his shoulder and sigh, letting the moment linger. Then I tilt my head up to see his face. Damien doesn't keep secrets from me—not anymore—and I expect him to tell me what the phone call was about. But he says nothing, and my stomach twists miserably. Because I understand Damien well enough to know that the only reason he'd hold back is to protect me. And right now, he's doing his damnedest to shield me from the emotional hell of this trip.

"Damien?"

He twines his hand with mine, then kisses our joined fingers. "I'm sorry. This is our time. Your time. I wouldn't have called back, except—"

"I get it. Really." And I do. I understand why he returned the call. And I understand that this apology is his way of telling me that he's not saying a word about it. Not now. Not until we've seen my mother.

"We should get going," I say.

For a moment, he holds my gaze, trying to measure whether I'm truly game-ready. Then he nods and glances down at the phone. "Are you sure you don't want to call her first?"

"No. Let's just go." What I don't say—but I'm sure Damien understands—is that there's a certain amount of appeal in the element of surprise. For once, maybe I'll have the upper hand. And the fact that Damien will be standing on her threshold with me is a bonus. I flash a small but very genuine grin. "I think you intimidate her," I say.

"Me?" His smile is wide and boyish. "I can't imagine why."

"Mmm," I say. "Okay, onward." I gesture regally, indicating he should pull back onto the road. He'd stopped in front of one of the stately homes just a few blocks away from Highland Park Village—one of the ritzier shopping areas in the country, and a place with which I'm very familiar. I'm pretty sure my mother bought everything from designer diapers to ball gowns for both my sister Ashley and me in the center's boutiques.

But despite the society page sheen of this Dallas enclave, a Phantom stands out. Especially this fully restored beauty.

"The neighbors are jealous," I say, nodding toward two women openly gawking at the car as they jog. "They're wondering who's moving into the neighborhood with more money than they have."

Damien brushes off the comment. "It's not the price that intrigues them," he says. "It's the beauty. The craftsmanship. The restoration. This is a neighborhood that thrives on appearances," he adds, nodding to his right and the line of elegant homes we are passing. Then he glances to his left, his eyes roaming slowly over me. "And this car—and the woman in it—are two things of pure beauty."

My cheeks warm. "I'll agree with you on the car," I say modestly, though I can't deny that the compliment pleases me. "But I think they're mostly fascinated with the man behind the wheel—and the fact that he's on the right side."

Usually when we're in a limo, Damien's personal driver, Edward, acts as chauffeur. But Edward's not with us on this trip, and even if he were, I know Damien would insist on driving his new toy.

It's odd being a passenger on the driver's side, but this 1967 Phantom V limo is as British as they come, having once been a formal royal family touring limousine.

No wonder I feel like a fairy tale princess.

We'd come to Dallas for my work, but when Damien had learned about the trip, he'd made an appointment to see a retired aerospace engineer he'd once met at a classic car show whose hobby-turned-second-career is restoring Bentleys and Rolls Royces to mint condition. We'd gone straight to his home in North Dallas after arriving, and Damien had spent two hours in a state of bliss talking about this Phantom.

"How much?" Damien had asked, after he'd inspected the limo thoroughly, commenting on the brilliant design and mechanical prowess with the kind of rapture that most people use when talking about movie stars. I couldn't deny that he was right about the car's beauty and uniqueness. It's painted a typical black, but the sheen is such that every angle and curve is set off to perfect advantage. And the interior is as elegant as a palace, the wood carved and polished to perfection, the leather seats soft and supple. The car is rare, too. Apparently, only five hundred and sixteen of this particular model were made.

The engineer quoted a six-figure price, and Damien pulled out his checkbook without the slightest hesitation. Less than an hour later, we were driving down the North Dallas Tollway in the latest addition to Damien's vehicular menagerie, and Damien's giddy expression reminded me of a little boy on Christmas morning.

Now, he maneuvers the limo through Highland Park, the well-heeled neighborhood in which I grew up. Though my family's net worth never came close to Damien's, we were hardly scraping by. My grandfather had made a fortune in oil, and though much of that was lost in the recession—and later by my mother's bad management—there's no denying that I was a child of privilege, just like every other kid living in these massive, tony mansions.

I'd walked away from all that when I moved to Los Angeles, intent on escaping my past. I'd wanted a new life, a new Nikki. And I'd been determined to make it on my own without my mother's baggage holding me down.

Now, I can't help but smile as I look at Damien. At this car that cost more than most people earn in a year. It's funny how things shift. I was wealthy in Dallas, but miserable. Now, I'm filthy rich in Los Angeles and happier than I could ever have imagined. Not because of the bank account, but because of the man.

"You're smiling," he says, sounding pleased, and I'm once again struck by the fact that he is as much on pins and needles as I am. Damien, however, isn't worried about seeing my mother. Damien is worried about me.

"I was just thinking how happy I am," I admit, and then tell him why.

"Because the money isn't the heart of what we are to each other," he says. "You'd love me even if I were destitute."

"I would," I admit, then flash an impish smile. "But I can't deny that I like the perks." I run my hand over the dashboard. "Of course, I'd like *this* particular perk better if Edward were here."

"Not satisfied with just holding my hand, Mrs. Stark?"

"I'm fine with hand holding for now," I say archly. "But later, I want more. Later, I want your hands on all of me."

The glance he shoots me overflows with heat and promise. "I think that can be arranged."

"Eyes on the road, driver," I say, then point. "And turn here."

He does, and immediately my mood downshifts. Because now we're on my actual street. Now, we're a few blocks away from my childhood home.

I draw a breath. "Almost there. And I'm fine," I add before he has a chance to ask. I'm not fine—not entirely—but I'm hoping that by saying it, I'll banish the hideous aching in my gut and the nausea that is starting to rise up inside me.

"Just tell me when."

I nod, and for a moment, I picture us driving past, just going on and on until we're out of the neighborhood, back in Dallas proper, and far, far away from the memories that are now washing over me like wave after wave crashing onto a sandy shore. Me locked in a pitch-black room because little girls need their beauty sleep, and Ashley whispering to me through the closed door, promising me that nothing is lurking in the dark to hurt me. A stylist tugging and pulling on my long, golden hair, ignoring my tears and cries of pain as my mother stands by, telling me to control myself. That I'm embarrassing her. My mother gripping my arm as she tugs me up the walkway to register for my first pageant, my eyes still red from the sting of her hand on my kindergarten-age bottom, a reminder that beauty queens don't complain and whine.

I think of a dinner plate with the tiniest portion of plain chicken and steamed vegetables while my mother and sister eat cheesy lasagna, and my mother telling me that if I want to be a pageant winner, I need to watch every calorie and think of carbohydrates as the devil. Then her mouth pursing in disapproval when I insist that I don't care about being a pageant winner. That I just want to not be hungry.

I was never good enough. Too chunky, too slouchy, too lackluster. Even with an array of crowns and titles, I never met her expectations, and I don't remember a time when she ever felt like mother or friend. Instead, she was the strict governess of stories. The wicked stepmother. The witch in the gingerbread house.

My older sister Ashley escaped her clutches by the simple act of not winning the pageants she entered. After several failures, my mother gave up. And though I tried to fail, too, I was cursed with crowns and titles.

For years, I'd thought that Ashley had the better end of the deal. It was only when she later killed herself after her husband left her, that I understood how deep Ashley's scars had run. Mine were physical, the self-inflicted scars of a girl who took a blade to her own skin, first to release the pressure and gain some control, then later to mar those pageant-perfect legs and end the madness of that horrific roller-coaster.

Ashley's wounds were under the surface, but still deep. And at the core, both mine and my sister's scars were inflicted by our mother.

My heart races, and I force myself to breathe steadily. To calm down. We're almost there, and if I'm going to see my mother, I need to be in control. Show even the slightest weakness, and she'll pounce on it.

And, yes, I've grabbed the upper hand before—I sent her back to Texas after she tried to take over planning my wedding, ignoring what I wanted in favor of her own skewed vision—but in Dallas she definitely has the home-court advantage.

"Nine-three-seven?" Damien asks, referring to the address, and I nod.

"The first house on the left after the bend," I say, and I'm proud of how normal my voice sounds. I can do this. More than that, I *want* to do it. Clear the air. Wash away all the cobwebs.

Basically, I'm doing the parental equivalent of burning sage in a house tainted with bad memories.

The thought amuses me, and I'm about to tell Damien when the car rounds the bend and my humor fades.

Moments later, my childhood home comes into view. But it's not my mother's Cadillac parked in the drive. Instead, I'm staring at two unfamiliar Land Rovers, a Mercedes convertible, and a moving van.

So where the hell is my mother?

2

A chill cuts through me, a cold sweat breaking out over my whole body as Damien eases the limo in behind the van, then kills the engine.

I turn to him, searching his face for the answers I need, but of course he doesn't have them. And for one quick, horrible moment, I'm overwhelmed by the sensation of being swept out to sea, pulled away from everything warm and safe until I am cold and alone and drifting without anything to anchor me.

Outside the car, a little boy of about four runs across the lawn toward us, his eyes wide. A woman who's probably five or six years older than me hurries behind, calling for him to stay away from the car.

I watch the boy, as mesmerized by him as he is by the Phantom. Then his mother reaches him and swings him around, making him laugh before she settles him on her hip, and he snuggles close, his thumb going into his mouth.

I exhale, only then realizing I'd been holding my breath.

"Come on," Damien says gently, reaching for his door.

"But she's not here."

He brushes a lock of hair off my cheek, the touch as sooth-ing as his voice. "But the house still is."

He's right. I'd been focusing so hard on my plan to see my mother that I hadn't thought about the other memories that surrounded her. Memories made inside the walls of this house. I think of Ashley, who would now be about the same age as that young mother, and suddenly I want nothing more than to see the room that had once belonged to her. "You're right." My voice is thick with the tears I'm determined not to shed. "Do you think we can go in?"

"We'll go in," he says in the same firm, confident voice I've heard in both the bedroom and the boardroom. Immediately, I relax, because no matter what else went wrong today, I am cer-tain that somehow, someway, Damien will get me inside that house.

He gets out, then circles the car to open my door. It's early summer, and a wall of Texas heat slams into me, overwhelming the lingering cool inside the air-conditioned car. Damien helps me out, and by the time he shuts the door behind me, the mother and her son have reached us.

"May I help you?" Her voice has the clipped, polished tone of someone raised in the northeast.

"I—I'm Nikki Fairchild," I say, figuring that under the cir-cumstances, she'll recognize my maiden name. "I was looking for my mother," I add lamely when she just stands there, appar-ently not recognizing the name at all.

"Your mother?" Her nose crinkles in confusion.

"Elizabeth Fairchild," Damien clarifies. "She owns—or used to own—this house."

"We just closed on it yesterday." On her hip, the boy squirms, and she lets him slide down her leg, where he stands clinging to her like she's the safest haven in the world.

"Do you know how long the house was on the market?" Damien asks as the little boy inches toward the Phantom.

Her forehead furrows as she studies Damien. "Wait. I know you. You're that tennis—"

"Nikki?"

Another woman's voice cuts her off, and I jump a bit. Both at the sound of my name and at the familiarity of the voice. I look toward the house, and my heart leaps at what I see. The woman on the porch is cast in shadows, but I recognize her instantly. "Mrs. McKee?"

I hear the tremble in my voice, but I don't care. I launch myself forward, and by the time I cross the lawn, she's stepped off the porch and is hurrying to meet me. I fling myself into her arms and let her wrap me in a tight, loving hug. I soak it in, the affection and support from this woman I've known my whole life, and who, for so many years, I'd pretended was my real mother. I'd dreamt that sooner or later I'd learn the truth, and Ashley and I would move in with her family. Because how the hell could Elizabeth Fairchild really be anyone's mom?

When we finally break apart, my cheeks are wet with tears. Damien is beside me again, and I reach out. He takes my hand automatically, then nods at Mrs. McKee. "You must be Ollie's mother," he says, referring to my childhood neighbor and one of my two closest friends.

"Please, call me Caroline. And you're Damien, of course."

"Oh! That's it! You're Damien Stark!"

"This is Misty," Caroline says, gesturing to the excited young mother. "She and her husband just moved from New Hampshire. I've known her father for years."

"It's a pleasure to meet you both," Damien says, as Misty's jaw hangs open.

"I can't tell you how happy I am to finally meet you," Caroline says to Damien. "And it's been far too long since I've seen you, young lady." She beams at me with the kind of sincere affection I've never seen in my own mother's eyes. "I had no idea you were in town."

"I didn't think to tell you," I admit. "I didn't even tell Ollie I was coming to Texas. I'm here for business. I have a meeting tomorrow and—" I cut myself off, frowning. "The truth is, I came here to see my mother. Do you know where she moved?"

Caroline shakes her head. "We didn't stay in touch once Arthur and I downsized to our condo in University Park. It's just a few miles, but it feels like the Grand Canyon. But I heard through the grapevine that she wanted a smaller place, too, and when I learned that the house was on the market, I mentioned it to Misty and her husband. That was about two months ago, wasn't it?"

Beside her, Misty nods. "We only dealt with our real estate agent, though. And the house was already vacant when we first saw it."

"Mama! Mama!" Her little boy tugs on her hand. "Car! Please! Wanna see the big car!"

"Hush, Andy." Misty's voice is as gentle as her smile, but when she looks up at me, it's confusion I see on her face. "Your mom didn't tell you she moved?"

"She's probably in one of those corporate apartments, waiting for her new place to be ready and didn't want to bother you with a temporary address." Caroline's off-the-cuff explanation comes easily, but the tension around her eyes reflects both understanding and commiseration. Because the truth is, Caroline knows more details than most about the rocky relationship between my mother and me. Not that I ever told her—and not that she ever said a word to me—but I'm certain that Ollie shared some of what I'd confessed to him. And I will be forever grateful for the times that Caroline let me stay late at her house under the guise of doing homework, or when she fed me a Hershey's bar and made me promise to keep it a secret because if word got out, all the neighborhood kids would want one.

In other words, I am certain that Caroline knows damn well that the thought of keeping me up to date never crossed my mother's mind. As far as Elizabeth Fairchild is concerned, I'm a prop, not a daughter. If she needs to use me, she'll contact me. Otherwise, out of sight is very much out of mind.

I know it shouldn't bother me. After all, I don't want that woman in my life. And yet, as I look at the tender expression on Misty's face as she kisses her little boy's forehead, I can't deny the overwhelming sense of loss that washes over me.

But how the hell can you lose what you never even had?

"We can always give Elizabeth a call for her new address," Damien says dismissively, as if we call my mother all the time. "To be honest, we came mostly for the house. I've never seen Nikki's childhood home," he adds, and I'm absurdly grateful that he didn't tell these women the truth: that it's me, not him, who's driving this train. That I want—no, *need*—to see the inside of the house I grew up in. A house that was never a home. And maybe, just maybe, if I walk through it one last time, I can finally, truly leave it behind.

Damien flashes Misty the kind of smile that always makes me go weak in the knees. "Since we're here, I wonder if we could go inside?" When she hesitates, he nods toward the Phantom. "While we're in there, feel free to let that little guy check out the Rolls."

"Oh!" Her eyes go wide, then she smiles and looks down at the child, who's plunked himself on the grass and is poking at the ground with a stick.

Damien squats down so that he's almost eye-level with the boy. "What do you say, Andy? Want to go take a look inside the big car?"

His eyes go wide as he looks up at his mother and then to Damien. Then he nods slowly, apparently afraid that if he shows too much enthusiasm, we'll all laugh and tell him we were just kidding.

"He's adorable," I say, then grin as Damien stands up again beside me. "And he looks like a handful."

Misty laughs. "You have no idea. Or maybe you do?" she looks between the two of us curiously. "Any kids?"

"Not yet." I flash my Social Nikki smile. "But we have a niece about his age and a nephew who's coming up on two."

Caroline rests a hand on her hip. "Well, I think you need to get busy," she says. "I'd love to be Auntie Caroline. Goodness knows Ollie's isn't making any progress toward giving me grandchildren."

"Someday we will," Damien says as he slides his arm around my waist.

"I certainly hope so." Caroline smiles fondly at both of us. "You two would make beautiful babies."

"I can't argue with that," Damien adds, as he pulls me closer and presses a kiss to my temple. "Nikki's going to make an incredible mom."

I tense, my demeanor shifting from socially friendly to icily polite. This isn't a conversation I want to have right now. Not with a stranger. Not with Caroline. Not even with Damien, and I'm frustrated that he so seamlessly slid into the role of eager father. We've talked about this over and over, and I'd thought we were on the same page. Someday, yes, I want to hold our child in my arms. But neither of us are ready for kids yet. There are too many barriers, too many challenges. And the fact that he's now speaking so cavalierly about something so important makes my insides twist up. Especially since I can hardly call him out while we're standing on a lawn in Dallas and I'm so goddamn vulnerable already.

Fuck.

I pull out of his embrace, and when I do, Damien catches my eyes. I see the apology on his face, but I'm not in the mood. I'm too off-kilter as it is, and so I just shove my hands in the pockets of my summer skirt. For a moment, I think he's going to say something else, but then he turns his attention back to Misty and tells her that the car is unlocked.

As they speak, I head toward the house with Caroline beside me. With each step, my feet feel heavier and my pulse quicker. It's silly, I know—it's not as if I'll find my mother lying in wait—but I haven't been back in this house in years, and now that I'm about to walk inside, I'm positively crackling with nerves. I want Damien beside me. I want his hand in mine. And I'm angry and hurt and pissed that just a few little words have dropped a wall between us. Angry at him. And, yes, angry at myself, too.

Behind us, I hear Misty speaking to Damien. "I'll wipe off his hands before he gets in the car. And feel free to look around as much as you want. It's kind of a maze in there, though. We haven't unpacked a thing."

Caroline and I pause, and I watch as Misty hurries off after Andy, who's running as fast as his little legs will allow toward the Rolls Royce. Damien turns but hesitates before walking toward us, his expression unreadable. Then he cocks his head just slightly, and when his brows rise in inquiry, I see everything he's not saying aloud. *I'm sorry. Are we okay?*

The fist around my heart loosens, and I draw a breath, wait a beat, and then extend my hand. For an instant, relief flickers in his eyes. Then his expression clears, and he joins us, locking his hand with mine.

Caroline looks between us, then smiles so brightly that I have to wonder if she's picked up on the tension. Not that I'm about to ask. Instead, we continue to the house. "How many times did I walk you home when you and Ollie were little?" Caroline asks as we step onto the porch. "Or come over here to drag Ollie back home when you two spent the day in your pool?"

"A lot," I say, letting the memories distract me. The truth is that Ollie rarely came over here. When we were allowed to play together, we both preferred his house. Only in the dead of summer did we stay here to enjoy the pool, and then only after my mother had assured herself that I was covered head-to-toe with sunscreen. God forbid the beauty queen get a sunburn or freckles.

"Go on, sweetie," Caroline says. "I'll wait for you two out here."

I nod, and when Damien squeezes my hand in silent support, I realize how clammy my palms have become. The door is already ajar, so I use my free hand to push it open. I swallow and then, before I can lose my nerve, I step over the threshold.

I hesitate, not sure what I expected. Memory-shaped ghosts drifting down from the ceiling? My mother's face looking back at me from the hall mirror? Her voice ordering me to go to my room and rest because it's almost nine o'clock and I need my sleep before that weekend's pageant?

But there is nothing. It's just walls. Just tile and hardwood, paint and wallpaper. I feel my body relax, and when I meet Damien's eyes, the corner of his mouth curves up in a smile of understanding.

"Where was your room?" he asks as we move through the foyer to the open-style living area.

"That way." I point to the long hallway that leads off to the right. "My mom was in the master bedroom, all the way on the other side of the house. But Ashley and I were both down here."

"Show me."

"I doubt it's going to look anything like what it did when I was here," I say, but I'm already heading that way. I'm right, of course. The walls are a plain, flat white where they had once been a pale pink. I'd wanted lime green. Something funky and fun and a little bit obnoxious. A counterpoint to the so-good-they're-smarmy manners and perfectly proper clothes that had been foisted on me for my entire life.

My mother, of course, had vetoed that plan, because little girls who win pageants are the kind of girls who love pink.

Girls who follow the rules. Who don't make a fuss or cause trouble.

Girls who don't have opinions of their own.

At least that's what every word out of my mother's mouth seemed to imply. I've learned better since, and I know several women I respect who've done the pageant circuit. But back then, I had my mother in my head. And every time I won a pageant, I had to wonder what that said about me. Was I truly that boring and empty-headed? Was that really all I was good for?

I remember going to Ashley, curling up among the pile of pillows on my big sister's bed and whispering that I hated our mother. That I hated pink. That Mother was mean and I wanted my walls to be my walls and it wasn't fair and why couldn't I ever do anything I wanted, and on and on and on.

"Do you know what she did?" I ask Damien, after I've told him all of that. "She came home from school the next day with a tiny jar of lime green paint she'd swiped from the high school art department." I blink back the tears that have gathered with the memory. "She told me I needed some green, and so we painted a tiny green square right behind my bedside table, and then we took a pencil eraser and wrote our initials in the paint. It would have been right about here," I say, leading him to the far side of the room and pointing to a pile of boxes.

He bends, moves a couple of the boxes aside, and then crooks his finger for me to join him. I do, then suck in a breath when I see what he's found. It's been covered, but I can still clearly see the hint of a green square beneath the flat white. And in the middle—more texture than image—are the initials NF and AF.

My knees go weak, and I let myself slump to the ground, Damien's arms going around me to cushion my fall.

"Thank goodness you're here," I murmur, my back to his chest.

"I'll never be anywhere else."

I nod, acknowledging the simple truth that is the shining miracle of my life as I lean back against him, grateful for his warmth and strength.

"I don't want to remember," I admit. "And yet just being here—it's all coming back. Good. Bad. It's crashing over me like waves. All these memories, and I don't have the strength to stop them coming."

"Then don't," he says. "Let go, baby. Let the tide take you. I'll be your tether. I'll always pull you back home."

I squeeze my eyes shut, lost in the magic of his words. In the promise that he will always protect me. That he'll always love me.

A shiver cuts through me. Not from a chill. Not from fear. But from the simple realization that I should have known that kind of all-encompassing, unrelenting love from my mother. But I'd had to find it in my sister. In my friends.

In Damien.

"My mother didn't have a clue," I whisper. "Not even an inkling of how to be a mother."

The tears flow freely now as I recall the day I got the phone call that Ashley was dead. My mother's flat voice that she'd killed herself. And not flat with regret or mourning, but with disapproval. As if Ashley hadn't lived up to expectations.

The irony, of course, was that it was expectations and insecurities that had killed my sister. Her deep-seated certainty that she had no clue how to be a wife. That when her husband left her for another woman, it was proof that she was a failure—just like my mother had always said.

She'd killed herself because she'd believed she was nothing. But to me, Ashley had been everything.

"We were sitting here when she told me she was going to get married. On the floor beside my bed. And she said she was going to have a good life and be a better mom than ours."

My words tumble out as fast as my tears. I love Ronnie and Jeffery, my niece and nephew, but Ashley's child should have come first. I wanted so badly to be Aunt Nikki. To be the very best aunt ever, just like Ashley had said. "She never got the chance."

Suddenly, the loss of my sister is like a physical pain in my chest. I turn in Damien's arms, bury my face against his chest, and sob.

I'd come to this house wanting to exorcise my demons, but now it seems like the ghosts are everywhere.

I gulp in air, then try to force words out past my tear-clogged throat. "Please," I beg. "Please, can we just get out of here?"

"We're already gone." He kisses me gently, then takes my elbow to lead me out of the room. But I just stand there beside him for a moment, hating how weak and fragile I feel. I try to gather myself, determined to get out of this house without Caroline or Misty seeing any evidence of pain on my face.

And yet I can't manage. My knees are weak. My skin clammy. I start to take a step to the door, but the world seems to turn inside out, and me along with it.

I have only enough time to look up at Damien—to see the worry etched on his face—before the grayness takes over, and I collapse into my husband's arms.

3

"Nikki!"

Damien's voice—tense, afraid—seems to wrap around me.
Something tangible that, maybe, I can cling to. That I can use
to pull myself back.

"Sweetheart? Baby? Come on. That's it. You can do it."

I feel the warmth of his body surrounding me. Cradling me.
His words are soft with encouragement, but the gentleness only
hides an undercurrent of fear. I imagine his face in front of me,
coming in and out of shadows.

Then I realize that it's not my imagination. Instead, my eyelids are fluttering open, my body trying to return to normal
even though my mind is still lost in this odd netherworld where
time seems so painfully slow and Damien's arms so deliciously
warm.

"That's it, baby. You're going to be fine." I see the worry that
tightens the lines around his mouth. That sharpens the amber
of one eye and transforms the onyx depths of the other into a
hopeless abyss. Then he turns to speak to someone else, his
voice low and strained. "Where the hell is the damned
ambulance?"

"On its way. I think I can hear the siren." Caroline stands behind him. Her brow is furrowed, and she's twisting her hands. Farther back, Misty clings to her little boy, her expression pinched, and I wonder if she is concerned about me or about what her new neighbors will think.

I hear the approach of sirens, too, and despite the summer heat, my skin prickles from the ice water that suddenly floods my veins, the chill pushing me all the way into consciousness. With a vague sense of wonder, I realize we're back on the front lawn. But I have no idea how we got here.

"What happened?" My voice is raspy, but it's enough to send relief washing over the three faces around me.

Carolyn steps forward, and though she puts her hand on Damien's shoulder, her eyes are on me. "Nikki, sweetie, it's going to be okay. It's probably just the heat. Nothing to worry about at all."

I try to push myself more upright. It's harder than it should be—I'm light-headed and unsteady—and when I see fresh worry on Damien's face, I stop trying and simply let him hold me. "I fainted?" Of course, I did, but the thought is so startling that I can't help but state the obvious as a question.

"You scared the crap out of me," he says.

"I'm okay now." I speak firmly, as if saying the words will make them true. Then I try to shift to my knees so that I can push myself all the way up to standing, but Damien holds me down.

"No, you don't." He holds me firmly in place. "Sit and rest until the ambulance gets here."

I grimace at the thought of being examined here on Misty's landscaped front lawn. "Honestly, it's not like I got bit by a rattlesnake or suddenly came down with Ebola. I just got light-headed. It's no big deal."

"It is to me," he says, and with those simple words, my argument dies on my tongue. I'm fine—I know that I'm fine—but

Damien needs the reassurance, and I'm willing to do whatever it takes to fully erase the fear from his eyes.

Unfortunately, after being poked and prodded and monitored by two efficient paramedics, we don't have a definitive explanation for my fainting spell, and worry still lines Damien's face.

The only upside is that they don't insist that I go to the hospital, but they do want me to see my own doctor soon, as my blood pressure is low enough for concern.

Damien thanks them, then starts to type something out on his phone as I watch them pack up and return to the ambulance. They pass Misty, who has moved to the driveway and is talking with three curious neighbors and, probably, cursing the moment Damien and I darkened her doorstep.

"Do you want some juice?" Caroline asks. "I bet Misty has a cooler of juice boxes. Or I can run to the market."

"No, really, it's fine. But thank you. I think you're right. I'm not used to the heat anymore." This time when I start to get up, Damien helps me, his phone now back in his pocket. "I'll go see my doctor when we get home just to be sure," I add, certain that Damien just sent a text to his assistant, asking that she schedule that very appointment for the second we return to LA.

"Actually, we're going now," Damien says. "There's a walk-in clinic just a few miles from here."

I, however, am done being Invalid Nikki. "The hell we are. I'm standing. I'm walking. See?" I circle him to prove my point as Caroline graciously moves toward Misty, obviously wanting to avoid getting caught up in a marital power struggle. "I probably just need food and air conditioning. So let's go get some lunch and then head back to the hotel so I can work on tomorrow's presentation."

"After the clinic. No—" he continues, cutting off my protest. "I want to make sure you're okay."

"Dammit, I am. I was just light-headed. How many times do I have to say it?"

"You were out cold for a full minute, baby. You didn't even stir when I carried you out here."

"But I'm awake now." I force myself to take a mental step back. To breathe. I don't like doctors. I never have. My memories of doctors are tied up with my mother's ploys to get me prescription appetite suppressants because "she's such a pretty girl, but her hips and thighs have a tendency toward chubby," or my own attempts to hide my self-inflicted scars, always fearing that some doctor would notice and insist I see a shrink.

"How about a compromise?" I suggest. "Hotel now, but if I start to feel dizzy, we'll go to the clinic."

For a moment, he says nothing, and I imagine the debate raging in his head. His desire to please me versus his concern and his need for answers. Finally, though, he nods. "All right, Ms. Fairchild," he says, using my maiden name as a term of endearment. "It looks like we have a deal."

I return the smile, feeling smug. Then I take a step toward Caroline and Misty, intending to say goodbye. And that's when my smugness vanishes.

That's when the nausea consumes me.

That's when I bend forward in a sudden, unexpected spasm and vomit all over Misty's pristinely manicured lawn.

4

"Considering I'm not sick, I'm certainly being pampered." We're back from the clinic Damien dragged me to, and now I'm curled up on our hotel suite's overstuffed sofa, my feet in his lap. It's barely past noon, but the curtains are closed, and the lamps are dim, and the ambience is making me sleepy.

He chuckles, then squeezes my big toe. "Are you saying I shouldn't be pampering my wife?"

"Actually, that was more of an 'I told you so' sort of comment." I conjure a victorious grin. "The pampering is my reward for being right."

He presses his thumbs against the bottom of my foot in a way that has me arching back and moaning with pleasure. "I'm always happy to reward you," he assures me. "But your prognosis is still an open question."

"I'm fine," I insist because I refuse to believe that anything is wrong. "The doctor said what I said—everybody gets lightheaded sometimes."

"And I get worried sometimes." He stands, shifting my feet onto the cushion as he does. Then he sits again on the edge of the sofa right beside me, his palm on my cheek. Slowly, he leans in, then brushes a gentle kiss over my lips.

A soft tremor runs through me, and I curve my hand around the back of his neck, prepared to pull him down for a deeper, more enthusiastic kiss. "You don't need to worry," I whisper.

"I promise I'll stop when he calls with the results of the blood work."

I hesitate, my building desire warring with a lingering frustration, and I let my fingers fall away as I exhale sharply.

Damien sits up, his brow furrowed. "What's wrong?"

"Nothing," I say automatically. But my pleasant mood has disintegrated, and I continue, "I don't like being under a microscope. But you're determined to keep pushing it." I shift to sit up, and in the process, give him a small shove. He looks at me with concern, his brow furrowed, and that only sparks my growing foul mood. "I just want to sit up," I snap.

He stands. "By all means, sit however you like."

I know I'm being bitchy, so I open my mouth to apologize, but that's not what comes out. "You're annoyed because of how I'm sitting?" My stomach twists unpleasantly. We fight—we're married, of course, we fight—but usually there's a reason. This one is all on me. I'm a mess, and I know it. My emotions have been all over the place today, and now something hard and hot is rising inside me, and it seems that I can't control my temper, much less my words.

Damien drags his fingers through his hair, his expression a mix of both compassion and frustration. "Baby, I'm sorry. This town. Your mom. Getting sick. You have every right to feel off."

"I'm not sick—I mean, come on, Damien, are you even listening to me?" Now it's my turn to stand. I tell myself I should leave, because everything inside me is churning. I'm touchy and emotional, and I know that no matter what he says, it's going to be the wrong thing, and that's never how I feel with Damien.

Which means he's right, of course. This is because of my mom. Because of Dallas.

And because I fainted and then vomited all over the lawn of a perfect stranger.

Just the memory makes me want to curl up and hide. "You put me on display," I accuse. "Calling an ambulance just for a fainting spell? The whole neighborhood came out to stare."

"Christ, Nikki. You passed out. I was fucking terrified. I wasn't concerned with being subtle."

"You weren't subtle at all." I choke a little, then blink furiously to hold back the tears. "What the hell happened to the Damien Stark who holds his private life close to the vest?"

He cocks his head, his eyes narrowing as he studies me. I meet his gaze, but hug myself, readying for the onslaught of accusations. That I'm overly emotional. That I'm tired. That I'm stressed. That I'm a complete emotional wreck because of this town, and maybe I should think about only competing for contracts that send me to cities that aren't Dallas. Better yet, that aren't in Texas.

He doesn't say any of that. Instead, he moves closer. He doesn't touch me, however, and as we stand there, only inches apart, I realize that I am longing for him to do just that. I want him to enfold me in his arms. I want to cling to him until the world turns right again. Until *I* turn right again.

But all he does is watch me. Then he says, "This isn't about fainting. It's not about being sick."

"It's not? Well, then by all means, tell me what it is that's upset me since you know me so much better than I know myself."

"It's about what I said to Caroline. About having kids someday."

I take an involuntary step backward. Because he's right. I hadn't realized it until he said it, but he's absolutely right. We've talked about kids a lot recently. We had the conversation before we got married, of course, and again more recently. And we've always been in agreement that we want to wait. That he's too busy being a master of the universe and I'm working long hours to get my own business off the ground. And on top of all of that, neither of us have good role models for how to be a parent. We'd agreed that we needed time. For ourselves. To get our lives in order. To get my business rolling.

But lately, I can't help but wonder if the expression of joy I see on Damien's face when he plays with our niece and nephew doesn't also have an element of longing. If he regrets waiting and wants to start a family of our own, just like Sylvia and Jackson have.

"Someday," Damien repeats, apparently following the bread-crumbs of my thoughts. "That's all I said to Caroline. Not today. Not next week. But someday." He takes my hands. "That's true, isn't it?"

I swallow, wishing I could read his mind as well as he always seems to be able to read mine. "Just because it's true doesn't mean it's not private."

Something hard flashes in his eyes, and for an instant, I think that I've pissed him off. But then he curses softly and shakes his head, his expression as warm as I've ever seen it. "You're right," he says, and I realize it's not me he's angry with; it's himself. "Goddammit, you're absolutely right. Sweetheart, I'm sorry."

"It's okay." His apology is like a ladder by which I can climb out of my deep, black hole. "Really." I draw a breath, realizing I'm no longer itching for a fight. That, somehow, he has smoothed my rough edges. "I just . . . I didn't expect it. I mean, we don't know Misty. And even though Ollie's mom's like family—"

"I get it," he says, leading me back to the couch. "You're right. And I love you. And I'm sorry."

He sits again, then pulls me down next to him. I sigh,

reveling in the easy way his arm goes around me. The comfortable rhythm of being curled up against him. "I'm sorry, too," I whisper. "You're right about my mom and all the rest. It put me in a really crappy mood."

"I'd be surprised if it didn't. So here's the question I have for you." His voice is so serious, I shift in his arms so that I can see his face more clearly. "Comedy or drama, movie or television?"

I shake my head, amused. "Don't you have to review some spreadsheets before your call about that production facility?" Damien wasn't planning to work this weekend, but the construction manager of one of his foreign plants called right before we left Los Angeles. There's some sort of crisis that needs to be dealt with first thing Monday, local time. With the time difference, that means Sunday afternoon in Texas. "And aren't I supposed to be prepping for my meeting tomorrow?"

"My call's not for another two hours," he says. "And if you do any more prep work, your head's going to explode." I open my mouth to protest, but he continues on. "Take a break. Chill with your husband. We'll have a late lunch, and you can spend all evening going over your notes. Sound like a plan?"

"So long as I don't have to pick what we watch." I yawn as I snuggle close, certain he'll choose something amazing because he always does. And, in fact, I enjoy the first hour or so of Audrey Hepburn's and Cary Grant's shenanigans in *Charade*. I can't speak to the rest of the movie, though, because the next thing I know, I'm prone on the sofa, disoriented as I wake from an unexpected nap.

Damien's voice drifts back from the bedroom area, and the television is off. I reach for my phone to check the time and notice that Damien's notes are no longer on the coffee table. Which explains why I hear him talking to someone—he must be on his conference call.

I sit up and stretch, fighting both frustration and worry. It's far too early for me to be this tired, and yet I've been dragging for over a week now. Even before we left LA, it was often all I could do to focus on my computer screen at work, and coding often felt like slogging through a pudding-filled swamp. I would load up on coffee, but I think I've finally OD'd on my favorite pick-me-up, because lately even the thought of downing a cup leaves me vaguely queasy.

In other words, I'm off my game, and that's both frustrating and a little nerve-wracking. I'm hardly ever sick, but what if this time there really is something wrong with me? I'd told Damien I was fine, but that was more because I wanted it to be true, not because I'm certain. A walk-in clinic wouldn't make me hang around for something like cancer. They'd let me go home, call with the bad news, and tell me to make an immediate appointment with a doctor in LA.

I stand, propelled off the couch by the warring forces within me. One side telling me to stop worrying, that everything I told Damien about me being fine is absolutely true. The other side arguing that I've felt off for weeks, and that, obviously, something is wrong, and I shouldn't have been so snippy with Damien since he's obviously right.

I scowl at my phone, not sure if I want it to ring so that I get the bad news, or stay silent so that I can hold onto the fantasy that all is well for just a bit longer.

Then again, maybe I should toss the thing off the hotel balcony, because clearly I'm turning into a raging hypochondriac, and that really can't be good.

Since none of the options sound appealing, I'm about to head into the kitchen to scope out the mini-bar. At home, I have an emergency stash of frozen Milky Ways, but I'd be happy for even the thawed kind at the moment.

I don't even get one step before my phone vibrates on the table, signaling an incoming call. I snatch it up, then sag onto the couch when I hear Dr. Cray's voice asking for me.

"This is Nikki," I say. "Am I—I mean, is there something wrong with me? Am I sick?"

"Actually, Mrs. Stark, you're quite healthy."

I draw a deep, grateful breath, then immediately frown. "Are you sure? The dizziness. And I've been so tired lately. Nauseous, too."

"Your dizziness was caused by the rapid drop in blood pressure, as I—"

"Exactly," I say. "But why's my blood pressure off? Please. If something's wrong, just tell me and get it over with."

"Slow down. All the symptoms you've reported are perfectly normal."

I shake my head. "No. No, they're not. Believe me, Dr. Cray, I know how I usually feel, and this isn't right. I'm not someone who falls asleep in front of the television before nine o'clock, much less just after noon. And dizziness? That's just weird. Trust me, this isn't normal. I've never felt like this before."

"I imagine that's because you haven't been pregnant before." I can hear the smile in his voice. "Congratulations, Mrs. Stark. You're going to have a baby."

5

You're going to have a baby.

Dr. Cray's words fill my head, random sounds that I can't quite process and that leave me shaky and confused. I reach for the arm of the couch and hold on, trying to steady myself.

"A baby?" The word feels thick on my tongue. Heavy and unfamiliar. "But that can't be right. I can't be pregnant. I'm on the pill." I've been on birth control since I was fourteen and got slammed with debilitating cramps.

"I'm sure you know that not every form of birth control is one hundred percent effective. You're walking proof of that now, Mrs. Stark, because I assure you that pill or not, you are definitely pregnant."

"How far along am I?"

"Nine, maybe ten weeks based on the level of HCG in your blood."

"HG—what?"

"A hormone. After an ultrasound, your OB can give you a better idea of how far along you are. Since you gave permission, I spoke with your family doctor, and he's set you up with an obstetrics appointment next Monday."

I blink and nod, trying to process that information. I'm pretty sure that's not the way it usually works, and I can only assume that Damien's clout is behind this elevated level of medical service. "Um. Okay. Who—"

"His nurse is going to email you all the information. In the meantime . . ."

He continues to talk, but it's all just noise. Pregnant? How can I be pregnant? I try to think back to my last period, but the truth is, I've never paid much attention. I've always just dealt with it when it showed up.

Now I wish I'd tracked the days religiously.

Pregnant.

That word rattles around in my head some more.

I'm really going to have a baby? How can that be? I can't be a mother. I mean, I don't have the slightest clue how to be a mother.

"Mrs. Stark?" Dr. Cray's voice breaks through the chatter in my head. "I understand this is a surprise. Do you have any more questions for me?"

"I—" I lick my suddenly dry lips. "No. No, thank you."

We end the call, and I toss my phone on the couch, then just stand there staring at the cushion as I take deep breaths and try to wrap my head around this unwieldy new reality.

"Nikki."

Damien's voice is soft, barely audible, but it's strong, and I cling to that as I lift my head and turn to face him.

He's standing in the doorway between the living area and the hall to the suite's three bedrooms. There's no expression on his face at all, and I have no idea how long he's been there, or how much he heard. "What's going on? Was that the clinic?"

He takes a step toward me, and I see the worry break through the mask of control. "Are you okay?"

Am I? I honestly don't know. But all I say is, "I'm pregnant."

For a moment, he remains completely still, his eyes unreadable. Then a wild joy colors his face as he takes a step toward me. "A baby," he says, his voice filled with awe and wonder. Another step, then another, until he is right in front of me. I expect him to pull me into a hug. To kiss my face, my mouth. To hold me so tightly in his embrace that there's no room for fear or doubt.

But he does none of that.

Instead, he drops to his knees in front of me and presses a kiss to my belly. His shoulders rise and fall as he draws in deep breaths, obviously trying to control himself.

For a moment, he simply clings to me. Then he tilts his head back to look at me. "A baby? Really?" His voice is so thick with emotion that it chips away at the numbness that has overwhelmed me. "We're seriously having a baby?"

I manipulate my lips up into a smile. "Looks that way." I congratulate myself on sounding normal, because the truth is that I don't feel normal at all. Instead, I'm nervous and stressed and twitchy, and I hate it. Because I should be basking. I should be lost in Damien's arms, lost in this once-in-a-lifetime moment.

Instead, I'm numb.

Instead, I'm terrified.

"Nikki?"

"It's okay." Hot tears pool in my eyes. "Really, I'm—"

That's as much as I get out before the sob escapes and fat tears trail down my cheeks. I'm not even tethered to the earth right now. I'm just a wash of jumbled emotions, twisting so fast I can't even process them. Shock. Joy. Fear. Excitement. Surprise. Terror. Happiness. All battering against me, leaving me overwhelmed and numb and not at all certain that this can really be happening.

"Sweetheart. Oh, Nikki, sweetheart." Damien is on his feet in an instant, and he pulls me close and strokes my hair. "Hey, hey, talk to me."

I want to—dear God, I want to—but my words are trapped behind a curtain of tears. I gasp, trying to relax as Damien rubs my back, making soothing noises. "I—I'm sorry," I manage. "It's just—I don't know. Hormones, maybe. I'm a mess."

"Sweetheart." The word is cut short by his kiss. So soft and gentle, I think I might melt. And when he finally pulls back, his expression is so tender it almost brings me to tears all over again.

He takes a seat on the couch, then settles me on his lap. I snuggle close, craving his strength and the safety of his arms. I want him to hold me tight. I want him to strip me naked. To touch and to tease.

I want him to make love to me. More than anything, I want to bury the quagmire of thoughts and fears dancing in my head under a blanket of passion.

"I love you," he says, and only when he uses the pad of his thumb to wipe away a tear do I realize that I've started crying again.

"I'm okay," I say, sniffling. "Damn hormones."

I'm still wearing the skirt I'd put on this morning, and he strokes his fingertips lightly over my bare leg, then brushes his lips over my shoulder. I shiver, craving a much more intimate touch and the oblivion that I know surrendering will bring.

Except I don't really want oblivion. I don't want to hide. Not from Damien—never from Damien.

And yet there is no denying that I'm doing exactly that. I'm closing off. Curling in on myself.

It's not a celebration I want, but escape, and I hate that my traitorous emotions are destroying what should be a moment of romance and joy.

I swallow, then push off his lap. "Bathroom," I say, then rush across the suite to the master bath.

I close the door, sit on the edge of the Olympic-size tub, and just breathe.

A moment later, Damien comes in. I lift my head, blinking as I look at him through tear-filled eyes. "I'm so sorry," I whisper.

He doesn't reply. Instead, he kneels on the thick pile of the mat laid out in front of the tub. He rests one hand on my thigh, then cups my cheek with the other. For a moment, we just look at each other, and I wish that we could stay like that forever. That we didn't have to speak or think or talk.

"You're overwhelmed," he says. "Your emotions are all over the place. You're happy. You're scared. You're confused."

I nod, blinking furiously so that maybe I won't start crying again.

"Mostly, you're hurt. And maybe just a little bit angry at me. But, sweetheart, you're carrying my child—*our* child—so how could I feel anything but joy?"

"No. No, it's not that." But even as I say the words, I know they are a lie. He's right, goddammit. He's so fucking right. I wanted him to be lost with me. To be confused and overwhelmed.

I wanted it, because I can't stand knowing that even with Damien beside me, I'm completely alone.

"It's exactly that," he says firmly. "Do you think I don't see it? Nikki, sweetheart, you've been a part of me from the first moment we met. How could I not see the gorge that's opened between us?"

Those damn tears start flowing again, and I stand up, extricating myself from his touch even as I brutally wipe away the tears.

"We talked about this," I whisper, my back still to him. "We had a plan. A path." I draw a breath and wipe my running nose. Then I turn to face him, expecting to see an accusation in his eyes. Instead, all I see is love.

I press my lips together and try to fight back another wave of tears. "We agreed we weren't ready," I say. "Neither one of us.

And we talked about how it was important to me to get my business more stable. Hire some employees so the company can grow even if I take time off. Time," I stress. "More time to . . ."

I straighten my shoulders and meet his eyes. "I'm not strong enough, and we both know it."

"You are," he says simply.

"The hell I am." I yank my skirt up to reveal the scars that mar my hips and thighs. The concrete evidence of my weakness. Of everything in me that's broken and fragile.

"Dammit, Nikki, don't point to your past just because you're afraid of your future."

"But I *am* afraid." I take a step closer, a rising anger giving me strength. "That's part of why we were going to wait, remember? Or were all those conversations bullshit? Have you been coddling me? Worse, have you been lying to me? Pretending you were okay with waiting when you've been wanting to build our family all along?"

"Nikki, no—"

"I've seen you with Ronnie and Jeffery. I know how much you adore them."

He runs his fingers through his hair, looking as miserable as I feel. "I do. And I'll adore our children. But I never lied to you. I swear to you, baby, I was one hundred percent with you on our plan. But life never turns out the way you expect. You and I know that better than anyone."

I stand rigid, so overwhelmed by emotion I fear I'm going to implode.

"Sometimes it's a crisis when a plan goes wrong. But sometimes it's wonderful." Slowly—with the same care he'd use when approaching a wild animal—he moves to me and places his hand on my belly. "This," he says earnestly, "is wonderful."

I swallow, trying to process his words. His attention is locked on me, as if he is trying to read our future in the lines of my face. After a moment, his brow furrows, and I see the slightest hint of uncertainty flash in his eyes. "Are you . . . Nikki, I get that you're scared. That you were caught off guard. But is there more going on here? Are you thinking about—I mean, do you not want this at all?"

At first, I can't even comprehend what he's asking. Then the meaning of the words—so horrible and wrong—hit me with the force of a slap. "Not want this? Not want your child? No, Damien, no. How can you even ask that? You have to know that I—"

I squeeze my eyes shut and press my fingertips to my temples because, of course, he would think that after everything I've said. "No. *No*. It's just . . ."

"What?" he urges.

"I don't know how to explain, but having a baby with you . . . building a family with you. I want that more than anything."

"I believe you," he says, and I sag with relief at the pure simplicity and love that color his words.

"But I still feel numb," I say, sitting on the edge of the tub, "and I don't know why."

My eyes are welling up again, and Damien comes to sit at my side. "Of course, you know why. Because you're surprised. Unprepared. And," he adds, putting an arm around me, "because you're not sure you can handle it. But you can, baby. I promise you can." He takes my hand, then lifts it and gently kisses my palm. "Sweetheart, you're not your mother."

A hard knot forms in my gut, because Damien has cut straight to the crux.

"How do you know?" My voice sounds as small and fragile as I feel.

"I just do. And I'm brilliant, remember? All the articles say so."

I laugh, the tightness inside me loosening a bit. "You

definitely have your moments," I concede before he leans in to gently kiss me.

After a moment, he stands, then holds out his hand to me. I take it, and he leads me back to the living room, then gestures for me to sit on the sofa. I do, and he sits beside me, then leans forward and pulls open the drawer in the coffee table. "I was going to show you this at dinner," he says in what seems like a complete non sequitur. "I pulled it from my files before we left Los Angeles."

He passes me a photo, and I take it automatically, making a little "oh" sound when I see the image—me in a bathing suit on a stage at the Dallas Convention Center. "You really kept this?"

"How can that possibly surprise you?"

He's right. Once upon a time, I would have thought it odd. Now I know that Damien cherishes even the most random memories of the two of us together.

I run my fingertip over the image of me. We'd met for the first time when I was competing in the Miss Tri-County Texas Pageant, and professional tennis player Damien Stark was one of the celebrity judges. I didn't realize it at the time, but that day changed my life forever.

"You scared me," I admit.

His brows rise. "Did I?"

"Because of the way you made me feel. I didn't know you— hell, I barely talked to you—but those minutes in the green room with you were so vivid, I knew even then that they'd be burned into my memory."

"I felt the same."

I smile. I know that now, of course, but at the time, I'd had no clue that Damien thought of me as anything but another contestant.

"I was overwhelmed by the intensity of you. You enthralled me. And I swear that if you'd asked me, I would have run off with you, just like that girl at the end of *The Graduate*."

"I was sorely tempted, I assure you." He brushes his thumb over my lower lip. "Do you have any idea what I wanted to do back then? How I wanted to take you away from that reception, find a dark room, and touch every inch of you. I wanted to take you over the edge, Nikki. I wanted to feel you explode in my arms. And as I stood there by those damn tiny cheesecake squares, all I could think of was how you would sound screaming my name when you came in my arms."

"Oh, yes." I shiver as I think about it. "I wanted it, too. But it never would have happened. I would have walked away, slapped you across the face, even. I was too much under my mother's thumb. Too locked into seeing myself the way that she saw me, and I didn't have the courage to break away."

I'm no longer talking about running from Damien that night, and he knows it. I'm talking about escaping from the life I was trapped in. The world where I was a walking, talking Barbie doll, and my mother was the girl playing with her pretty, mindless toy.

"But you did find the courage," he says gently.

I swallow, thinking about the scars that mar my body. "A blade isn't courage."

"No, it's not. It was a tool—the strength was always there. And now you don't need the tool anymore, either. You're strong, baby. You know I believe it."

I sniffle and nod. It's true. He looks at me and sees strength. He believes in me even when I don't believe in myself. "I have the strength because of you," I say.

He shakes his head. "That's not true. But even if it is, so what? I'm right beside you, and I promise you, sweetheart, I'm not going anywhere."

6

"You're so beautiful," I whisper to the baby in the crib. I reach for her, moving her gently into my arms, and she blinks wide, blue eyes at me, her expression of utter love so like her father's it makes my heart sing with joy.

I want to hold her close and never let go.

I want to applaud her first steps, hear her first words.

Most of all, I want to keep her safe.

She is the most precious thing in my world—our child. *Mine and Damien's.*

Tears of joy trail down my cheeks. Because she's finally here with us, and it's true and it's right and it's perfect.

I don't know how I ever doubted. How I could ever have been afraid.

"You can't do this."

The harsh, familiar voice pulls my attention away from my daughter, and I look up, my blood running cold when I see the woman standing in the middle of the nursery, arms crossed, a stern expression cutting deep lines into her usually attractive face.

"Mother?"

"You can't do this," she repeats, her eyes darting down to where I'm cradling my daughter.

Except when I look down, the baby is no longer there. My arm is still crooked, but there is a deep, raw wound running the length of my inner forearm, blood oozing from wrist to elbow.

Terrified, I look up again, only to find my mother clucking her tongue.

"No!" I scream. *"I didn't do this."*

"Are you sure?" she asks, and I realize I'm not. I'm not sure at all.

I look around wildly, wanting answers. Wanting help.

But we are no longer in the nursery. We're in the kitchen. And in my other hand, I'm holding an aluminum can top, its jagged edge stained with blood.

"See?" my mother says.

I can't speak. I can only shake my head as I search the room, trying to remember what it is that I've lost. *"The baby!"* I finally shriek, as my blood falls in red splotches onto the pristine white floor. *"Where's the baby?"*

I'm standing at the sink, and I look out the window, only it's no longer a window, and we're no longer in the kitchen. Now, I'm on a balcony, leaning against a metal railing, and we're so high up the world below looks like a drawing, and I have no idea where we are because the earth is too far away and unfamiliar to recognize.

But then I see the baby tumbling through space toward the ground.

"Ashley!" I scream, reaching uselessly for my child.

"I told you," my mother says. *"Of course, she'll fall. Of course, you can't save her."*

"No!"

I dive off the balcony after the baby, but I'm too far behind her. And she's falling and falling and falling, and she's going to crash against the hard, horrible world, and there's nothing I can do. I can't reach her. I can't save her.

But then I see Damien standing on the earth below. He reaches out. He pulls her in, then holds her close.

He saves her, and I start to shake as sweet relief floods through me.

Then I realize the next harsh truth—he can't catch me. Not while holding the baby.

I screwed up. I lost our child.

Thank God Damien was there to catch her, but he can't save me, too.

And as the ground rushes closer and closer, I scream and I scream and I scream.

"Nikki! Nikki, baby, wake up!"

I blink, still sobbing as I slowly come back to consciousness in Damien's arms.

"Damien." My voice cracks on his name, broken by the weight of my emotions.

"Do you want to tell me about it?"

I don't. I don't even want to think about it. But I rub the back of my hand under my dripping nose and then draw in a long, deep breath. "She was there," I whisper. "My mother. And I was holding the baby—and, oh, Damien. She was perfect."

It's silly because I know it was only a dream, but my breath hitches as I tell him the rest. About the baby falling. The terror that filled my throat—so raw I can still feel the scream that was ripped from me in those last moments. And then my relief when Damien caught our child, even though I plummeted to the ground.

"It was just a nightmare," he says, holding me close.

I nod because I know that's true, but at the same time, it felt more real than even the news of my pregnancy in the first place.

With a frown, I curl up even closer to him. We're in bed, and the last thing I remember is lying next to him as we watched a new spy thriller that Damien rented off the hotel system. I recall the set up and a car chase, but nothing after that, and I realize that I must have drifted off, sucked once again into the pregnancy vortex and then down, down, down into sleep and dreams.

Now, a news program is playing on the muted television. Either the movie is over, or Damien got bored. But he's still in the same jeans and pale blue T-shirt, so I don't think that much time has passed. Certainly, it's not yet morning.

I don't nap well—I always wake up disoriented, and right now I'm still trying to get my bearings. I glance toward the window and see the city lights sparkling in the dark. "Is it late?"

Damien shakes his head. "Not very. You slept through the movie, but I promise you didn't miss much."

A hint of a smile brushes my lips. "Sorry. I didn't mean to fall asleep." I sit up, then scoot back so that I'm leaning against the upholstered headboard. I want to shake it, but the dream still lingers, and I clutch the sheet in my lap, twisting it in my hands. "It seemed so real," I whisper.

"But it wasn't, baby. Just thoughts. Just your mind sorting through everything." He shifts so that he's facing me, then cups my chin and tilts my head so that I have no choice but to look right at him. "But you're not your mother. And I will always—*always*—catch you."

I draw a breath and manage a wobbly smile. "I know," I say truthfully. "I guess I just woke up too soon."

"Or just in time. I'm here, aren't I? And you woke up in my arms."

I laugh and nod as my eyes well again with tears. I blink furiously to hold them back, then I slide my fingers into his hair and pull him toward me, my mouth closing hard over his. The kiss is raw and deep, but I want it deeper. I want the connection—physical, emotional. And I want his strength.

Most of all, I want to always feel the way I do in Damien's

arms. Confident. Loved. Strong enough to face the world. "We can do this," I say as I gently break the kiss. "Maybe it's not the best timing, but you're right. This is our child, and we can make this work. Can't we?"

"Hell, yes," he says, then kisses me hard and fast, his face shining with triumph. "You know we can. What can't we do when we're together?"

I'm crying openly now. Not in fear this time, but relief. And, yes, in joy. "I love you," I whisper.

"That's a good thing." His smile lights his eyes. "Because we're going to have a baby."

"Ashley." I tilt my head up to meet Damien's eyes. "In my dream, her name was Ashley."

Slowly, he presses his hand against my belly. "Ashley," he repeats. "It's perfect." He meets my eyes. "Of course, it might be a boy."

"True," I say, then flash a grin. "A boy like Damien Stark. He'll be a handful."

Damien laughs and kisses me. "He certainly would."

I'd changed into a tank top and yoga pants the moment we got back to the hotel, and now his hand slips under the tank, and the sensation of his palm against my bare skin sends shivers through me. Slowly, he eases his hand up my body, tracing the curve of my waist and then grazing over my ribs before cupping my breast. His thumb finds my nipple and begins a gentle, rhythmic caress that has me biting my lower lip as tendrils of wanton heat spread out through my body, firing my senses and making me whimper with longing.

"Nikki."

His eyes meet mine, and I see the tension in them. An unfamiliar hesitancy that I don't understand, because when has Damien ever hesitated where I am concerned? He has always been bold, taking what he wants—and what I so willingly give him.

I frown, wanting to ask him what's wrong, but before I get

the chance, his hand abandons my breast to slide back down, so it rests just below my bellybutton. "Is it okay?"

At first, I don't understand his words, spoken with such sweet tenderness. Then I realize that he's talking about the baby, and I smile, utterly charmed. I rest my hand on his, then start to ease it down beneath the stretchy waistband of my yoga pants. "Yes, please," I say sincerely, as a fiery need sparks inside me. "It's more than okay."

"You're sure?"

I can't tell if he's teasing me or truly uncertain. "I'm beyond sure," I promise him. "You. Hormones. I don't even know. I don't even care. But please, Damien. Please. I need to feel you inside me. Right now. I need it as desperately as I need to breathe."

"Do you?" he says, with a deliciously wicked gleam in his eyes. "I think we can do something about that."

I whimper a bit because the next thing he does is pull his hand out from under the band of my pants, which isn't exactly the direction I want him to be moving. But then he shifts on the bed until he is straddling me, and his hand is under the hem of my tank top, his palm warm against the curve of my waist.

With wicked slowness, he strokes my skin, the friction and the heat making me crazy. I arch up, my nipples straining against the thin material of my skimpy tank top. "Please," I beg.

"Please? Please, what?" His palms graze my ribcage until he reaches the swell of my breasts. I whimper, my skin so sensitive now that even a whisper of breath would shoot straight through my core, making me writhe with need.

"Please, yes," I say. "Please, fast."

His brow cocks. "Fast? Are you sure?" One thumb lazily teases my nipple as the other hand eases the tank higher until both my breasts are exposed. "Slow has its advantages."

He lowers his mouth, then teases my areola with his tongue. The sensation is incredible, and I bite my lip to keep from whimpering. Damien, however, is determined to drive me crazy, and while his mouth wreaks havoc above my waist, his fingers trail down, easing inside my pants to cup my sex.

I'm incredibly wet, and he strokes me in slow, gentle movements, never entering me, never teasing my clit. Just building me up. Making me crave. Making me *want*.

Making me so damn crazy that I arch my back more and gyrate my hips—silently demanding that he do more than just tease my breast and my cunt. I want his teeth on my nipple, his finger on my clit. Mostly, I want his cock inside me.

"Please," I beg when I can't stand it anymore. My entire body is on fire, and if he doesn't fuck me soon I'm going to be reduced to nothing more than cinders.

"Please," I beg again, only this time I reach down and fumble at the button on his jeans. I manage to get it unfastened, then slip my hand inside the denim. He's wearing boxers, and I stroke him through the soft cotton, gratified at the low, growling sound in his throat, and the corresponding way that his fingers slip inside me, just enough to tease. To make me want even more.

I ease my hand inside his boxers to find him hard and hot in my hand. He shifts his hips, the movement helping my effort to free him from both boxers and jeans. And as I slowly stroke his cock, he closes his mouth over my breast and sucks, tugging so hard that I feel a corresponding ache in my cunt, and my muscles clench with longing.

"Say it, baby," he murmurs. "Tell me you want me to fuck you."

"Yes," I say. "Please, Damien. Please fuck me. Hard," I beg. "Fast," I plead.

He doesn't make me wait. With one wild motion, he flips me over so fast it leaves me gasping. "On your knees," he orders as he yanks my yoga pants down, leaving my ass bare and exposed.

My head is down, my tank still bundled above my breasts,

now pressed against the cotton sheet. My rear is in the air, and he strokes my ass cheeks. I spread my legs, limited by the fact that the pants are still midway down my thighs. I'm so wet, and when he thrusts two fingers inside of me, I press my face to the mattress and moan.

"Is that what you want?" he asks, bending over so that I feel his weight on my back, and his erection teases me as he whispers in my ear.

"Yes." My voice is strained, my thoughts little more than *need* and *want*. "Please," I beg. "Please, Damien."

His tongue teases my ear, and I whimper as he whispers. "Yes, baby. God, yes."

He's still wearing the jeans when he enters me, first with shallow teasing thrusts designed to drive me crazy, then more and more until he's slamming hard inside me, the denim brushing erotically against me as he takes me hard, filling me completely so that I'm gasping, my hands fisted in the sheets, lost in this sensation of being so completely connected with him.

Again and again he thrusts, and my sensitive nipples rub against the sheet, adding to the sensation that my entire body is on fire, lost in an inferno of Damien's making.

His breathing changes and I can tell he's close when one of his hands leaves my hips to reach around and tease my clit. "Now, baby," he says, as an electric current skitters over my entire body, racing to culminate at my core.

I let myself go, surrendering to him, knowing I'd trust him to take me anywhere, and as I let go, the crescendo builds and builds until he repeats, "now," and everything shatters into an explosion of light and color, and I tremble from the force of it before collapsing into Damien's embrace, his arms around me holding me tight and guiding my way back to earth.

"I love you," he murmurs, then kisses my temple as I curl up next to him, our clothes still askew and our breathing hard.

We stay that way for what feels like forever, and my eyes are beginning to droop when his phone rings beside us.

"Just ignore it," I say, snuggling closer.

My cheek is pressed against the T-shirt he still wears, and I can feel the tension as he starts to reach for the bedside table. "Sorry," he says, then sighs. "I'm juggling a few crises, or else I'd silence the damn thing. Better yet, I'd pitch it in the trash."

I manage a lazy laugh, but it shifts to concern when he gently slides out from under me and stands up beside the bed. He buttons his jeans, then says, "Okay, Charles. Tell me what you've learned."

He turns to me and smiles, but the expression feels half-hearted, and when he heads out of the room, I sit up with a frown as I think about the previous call from Charles. A call that seems a lifetime ago, but was really only hours.

I slide out of bed, then slip into my robe and follow Damien into the living area. He's standing at the breakfast bar, his back to me. His elbow is on the counter, his head is resting on his hand, the phone right beside him. Even from behind, he looks fragile, and my heart constricts. *Fragile* is not a word that's usually in the Damien Stark lexicon.

"What's going on?" I say gently.

He turns, his face revealing nothing.

"Just putting out fires at work," he says.

I move to him, then hold out my hand as if in greeting. His brow furrows, but he takes it automatically. I shake it. "I'm Nikki Stark," I say as if in introduction. "We've met before. I'm the woman who knows you well enough to know when you're not telling me something."

"Nikki—"

"No." I drop his hand and step back, my arms crossed over my chest. "Whatever's going on, it's personal. And you're trying to protect me. First because of my mom. Now, maybe, because of the baby. But don't you get it, Damien? There will always be something. And that's not your call to make. You're my husband, dammit, and I want to be there for you. Hell, I *need* to be there."

He's watching my face, and his expression is such a mix of frustration and pain and love it would be amusing if it weren't so real.

"Damien," I press. "Please."

Finally, he nods. "It's Sofia," he says, and it's as if he's taken a fist and punched me in the chest. I take a physical step back, my hand rising to cover my heart, like that would be sufficient protection from her.

"What about her?" My words come out in a normal voice, and I'm so proud of myself. Sofia Richter is Damien's oldest friend—and she completely reviles me. All things considered, I'm not crazy about her, either. And that, of course, is a complete understatement. Just hearing her name now makes me wrap my arms around myself in a tight hug.

"I've gotten news about her most recent evaluation," he says. He's pronouncing his words carefully, watching my reaction, but I'm determined to be nothing but supportive.

"Oh." Not long before Damien and I got married, Sofia completely lost her mind. Her crazy had a catalyst—me—but it also had a cause. She and Damien had both been abused by his tennis coach, a man named Merle Richter, who also happened to be her father. Damien was strong enough to cope, but Sofia spiraled down, the mental illness that had always been there inside her, tugging her deeper and deeper into an abyss.

Damien's taken care of her ever since Richter died when they were both teenagers. And right now, she's in an institution outside of London receiving the best mental care his money can buy.

I clear my throat. "So how's she doing?"

"She's doing well," he says. "Exceptionally well, actually."

"Oh. Well, that's good. But what does Charles have to do with all of that? That's why he called earlier, too, right?"

He nods, but the gesture is slow, and I can tell this whole conversation is difficult. I don't back off, though; I want too badly to know.

"So?" I press.

"I wanted more information than the institution was giving us. More than just the official evaluations. So Charles coordinated an investigation for me. Used his resources to talk to the staff and people who have interacted with her around town on her free days. They even spoke with the other patients."

"And?"

"And everything backs up the reports. She's doing fantastic."

There's a heaviness to his words that surprises me. "And that's bothering you?" I ask.

He shakes his head. "No. No, of course not. I just—"

He cuts himself off, his eyes on my face before he turns away, his fingers going to massage his temples as if he's fighting a whopper of a headache.

"She's like a sister to you," I say gently. "But she tried to hurt me. So you're happy for her, but confused."

Saying that Sofia tried to hurt me is a bit like saying the Pacific is a big lake. Because it was so much more than that. She befriended me, pretending to be someone else entirely. She got close, and then she threw down the gauntlet, all with the aim of trying to get me to cut—or worse.

She wanted Damien—and as far as she was concerned, I was in the way.

The whole thing had been a nightmare, and though Damien had continued to pay for her care after she was committed, he'd cut off all contact with her. But I know he never stopped caring about her.

Now, his lips curve into an ironic smile. "Yeah," he says. "That about covers it."

"It's okay," I assure him. "I know you love her. Of course you're going to be happy she's getting better."

He closes his eyes and nods, his body a tight wire of tension.

I move closer and wrap my arms around him, and he pulls me close, holding me so tightly I almost can't breathe. After a moment, he releases me. "Thank you," he says simply.

I step back, studying his face, but whatever vulnerability had been there is gone. All I see now is the corporate executive. A man used to hiding his emotions. To not giving anything away.

I frown. "Is there anything else? It feels like there's something you're not telling me."

"No. No, baby, of course not."

I nod, but my stomach twists. Because the truth is, I don't believe him. And that bothers me. More than that, it scares me.

Because now there's a gulf between us. A small one, maybe, but it's there. And I don't know how to cross it. But I need to.

I can do this, I think, my hand resting on my belly. I know that I can.

But only with Damien beside me.

7

I'm awake before the sun—but not before Damien. I'm not sure that I've ever been awake before Damien on a work day, and as I slide out of bed, I wonder if that will change once the baby is in our lives. When I'm up at four with diapers and feedings, and my schedule is all switched around.

I sit on the edge of the bed and press my hand lightly against my belly, feeling a bit unsettled. I'm still nervous about the baby, but the fear has vanished, leaving behind the kind of uncertainty and anticipation that is normal for facing the unknown. Even that fear is tempered by my knowledge that wherever this path leads, I'm traveling it with Damien.

So it's not the baby that weighs on me—it's the lingering secret. Or, rather, it's my fear that there *is* a secret. Maybe Damien really did tell me everything about Charles and the calls and Sofia. Maybe. But it feels like he's holding something back. And I can only hope that he will tell me soon. That he is only trying to keep my head clear while we are in Dallas.

I stand, then reach for my robe, telling myself that has to be it—he knows how stressed simply coming here has made me. How nervous I am about the interview today. And now, with the news of the baby and the mystery of my vanishing mother, of course, he is trying to protect me. That's all. Of course, that's all.

And as Damien steps into the room with a cup of coffee in his hand and tenderness in his eyes, I have to believe that I'm right.

"Good morning, beautiful," he says, then hands me the coffee, followed by a kiss.

"The kiss I like, but I'm not so sure about this." I look mournfully at the cup.

"Decaf," Damien says. "All the taste, none of the buzz."

I pretend to pout. "I like the buzz." I raise the cup, smell the brew, and put it down on the side table in disgust. "Yeah, no. Who would have thought that I'd ever reach the point of not wanting coffee?"

Damien pulls me close and cups my ass with one hand. "We'll just have to make sure you're stimulated in other ways until the baby's born," he murmurs, then nips my earlobe, making me jump.

"Careful," I say on a laugh. "You'll make me late, and then I'll blame you if I don't get the contract."

"Can't have that." He kisses my nose as he backs off. "How are you feeling? Any morning sickness?"

"None at all." I frown, because yesterday, I'd been so overwhelmed by hormones and nausea that I'd passed out. So what's changed? "You don't think that's a bad sign, do you? I did some reading online last night, and all the articles say that morning sickness is healthy, and—"

"You're fine," he says. "And if it makes you feel better, I'm sure it will be back. Morning sickness comes and goes, doesn't it? And it's not always in the morning, either. So consider today a gift, since you have your interview."

I take a deep breath. He's right, of course. I need to not freak out about every little pain—or the absence thereof.

"Speaking of, your car will be here in about an hour. Why don't you go get dressed, and I'll order breakfast."

"Pancakes," I say firmly.

"No eggs?"

I usually indulge in fried eggs and bacon when we're in a hotel, but now I shake my head and smile happily. "I thought about it, but the idea alone makes me nauseous."

Damien laughs. "See? Now go get dressed."

I start to, then pause at the door and turn back to face him. "Why don't you come with me? You could wait in the lobby. We could get an ice cream later. Celebrate my achievement."

"Not a bad idea, but I have a few calls scheduled and working from here will be easier. Plus, I'd rather celebrate with something more interesting than ice cream."

"Oh," I say, and my already riled-up hormones start to flutter even more. "In that case, wish me luck today. Because I really can't wait to celebrate with you." I pause, then cock my head. "Although, if you're thinking pickles and ice cream, just be aware that I haven't crossed that line yet, and I'll be very, very disappointed if that's your idea of 'more interesting'."

"Noted," he says, obviously fighting a smile. "But when you do cross that line, just know that I'll cater to your every whim."

His words, so passionate and sincere, warm me. "You already do," I whisper. "You always have."

I'm still smiling an hour later when I'm dressed and fed and reviewing my notes in the back of the car Damien hired to schlep me around for the day. I have my laptop open on the seat beside me, a yellow pad in my lap, and I'm going over the original solicitation for bids from the company to make sure that I have talking points to cover each one.

I know that my pitch is spot-on; I spent well over a week proofing the thing, and several more weeks before that doing the actual work of putting the proposal on paper and making sure I didn't promise more than I could deliver, both in terms of technological prowess and manpower to make it happen.

Right now, Fairchild Development employs exactly one person—me. And if I get this contract, I'm confident that I can handle the work. But Greystone-Branch is a multinational consulting firm, and with their business locked in, I'd not only make enough off the contract to hire at least two developers, but my little company would also be settled more firmly on the map. Which would mean more customers. Which means more employees. And more income. And on and on and on.

Planning for the possibility of rapid growth makes me nervous, so all my projections on paper are conservative. But I've reviewed every nickel and dime and decision with Damien, and when a man like Damien Stark says that my overall plan for growing the company looks dead-on doable, then I'd be a fool not to at least be cautiously optimistic about my little company's chances.

I'm scribbling some bullet points on possible tweaks to the user interface I've designed when my phone starts to blare out The Dixie Cups' classic *Chapel of Love* at full volume.

"You are a such a brat," I tell my best friend Jamie after I've dug my phone out from under my backseat pile of papers. "I told you to take that ringtone off."

"Why would I do that? It works, doesn't it? You totally knew it was me."

I roll my eyes. She'd been completely wasted when she grabbed my phone and fiddled with my ringtones not too long before she and Ryan got married. "What's up?" I ask, making a mental note to change the ringtone myself.

"Not a thing." Her voice is bright. A little too bright.

I slump back against the leather upholstery and cross my arms over my chest. "Give it up, James," I order, using the familiar nickname. "I know you too well."

She exhales. "It's just that you're in Dallas." Her words are almost tentative. "I wanted to make sure you're okay."

"I'm okay. Thanks."

"Oh, please," she says. "That's what best friends are for." But there's still something odd about her voice.

"Jamie?"

She sighs. "Sorry. I'm just having one of those days. But you're really okay? It's not weird being home? You've been so obsessed about your mom lately."

"I haven't been obsessed," I correct.

Jamie's been with me at least once when I saw my mother in Los Angeles. Except it had to be my imagination. Because there is no reason for my mom to be in Los Angeles without wanting something from me. Even when she'd arrived unannounced to supposedly help with my wedding, she'd really been angling for a chunk of Damien's money. So I knew damn well that she wouldn't come to LA to simply watch me from a distance.

I'd told Damien after the first sighting. At the time, I'd been working on the Greystone Branch proposal, and he'd suggested that I was worried about coming to Dallas if I landed the contract. A reasonable theory, and one that I considered accurate when weeks went by without seeing her again.

The next time, though, the proposal hadn't even been on my mind. "Well, duh," Jamie had said when I'd met her for coffee and consolation. "I know exactly why you're seeing her."

I'd almost choked on my latte. "You do? Why?"

"Because you have mommy issues."

"Don't be absurd."

"Oh, come on. You and Damien have been together longer than Sylvia and Jackson. They have two kids, you and Damien have a cat. You adore Ronnie, that's obvious. But when you hold little Jeffery, you light up so much it's blinding. Damien's the same way. It's like you guys are primed to procreate."

"He's our nephew, and he's adorable," I'd said defensively because kids weren't in the cards for us. Not then. Not yet.

But she'd been right. About everything, really. And now I'm sitting here in the back of a hired car with my hand over my belly, wondering if my mother's been in Los Angeles all this time, and thinking about why I was so nervous about having a baby when clearly Damien and I are more than ready to make this work.

"—how did that go, anyway?"

I straighten, realizing that I'd zoned out. "Sorry. What?"

"Your mom," she says.

"Oh." I exhale loudly. "I think I was right all along."

"You went to see her, right? How did—" She was speaking over me, but she cuts herself off sharply. "Wait. What?"

"My mom's not here. She sold her house. She's gone, Jamie."

"So you really think she's been in LA all this time?"

I sigh. "I don't know. But at least that would mean I haven't been seeing things."

"Fuck."

"Yup," I say, because honestly, that sums up the situation nicely.

"Are you okay?"

I hesitate because what on earth am I supposed to tell her? The news about my mom is all mixed in now with the news of the baby, and even though I desperately want to share that with Jamie, I don't want to tell her from fifteen hundred miles away.

"Nicholas?" Her voice is firm, and she uses her nickname for me in emphasis. "Are you okay?"

"Yes. Yes," I repeat more forcefully. "Honestly, James, I'm great. Damien's here and—well, everything is fine. It's good. I'll tell you all about the trip when I get home. And, hey," I say brightly, because I am totally changing the subject, "was there some other reason you called?"

"I—what?"

"You just sounded weird when you called. Like there was something else on your mind."

"Oh! Well, actually, yeah. Um, you're still coming to the premiere on Friday, aren't you?"

Our friend Jane's book has been adapted into a movie, and the red carpet premiere is Friday at the Chinese Theater. "Are you kidding? Of course. Why wouldn't I be?"

"I don't know," she says vaguely. "I just wanted to make sure."

I frown. "You still sound weird. Is something wrong? There's not trouble between you and Ryan is there?"

"Are you kidding? I'm drowning in marital bliss. Apparently, to my husband, a wedding ring is an aphrodisiac. I mean, everyone said the honeymoon phase would be over by now, but they were so wrong. Seriously, I thought I was well-fucked before we tied the knot, but now I—"

"Got it," I say, cutting her off before I have a visual picture that I'll never be able to un-see. "Ryan's going early to oversee security, right? Do you want to share the limo with us?"

"Normally, I'd jump at it. But this time, I'm turning you down cold."

"Really?" I can't help but laugh at the tone of her voice. "Why?"

"Because this girl is going to be on the red carpet interviewing celebs as they come traipsing into the theater. Live on camera in a seriously awesome dress."

"Jamie! That's amazing!" Jamie's been working as the weekend anchor job for a local news affiliate, but she's been gunning to get out in the field and do entertainment reporting. To actually be on a red carpet interviewing A-listers is pretty much her dream come true.

Jamie's got the kind of A-list good looks that the camera adores. If the industry hadn't chewed her up and spit her out, I really think she could have made it as an actress. Fortunately, she got over the acting thing quickly, and she discovered she loves journalism. Especially if it involves reporting about Hollywood. But the fact that she loves it means she has something to lose.

"I know, right? Totally amazing. And I didn't even ask for this. I figured I had no chance—I mean, who starts with the red carpet? But they just plucked me out of the massive pile of desperation, dreams, and sweat."

I laugh. "I think they plucked you from a pile of talent."

"Pfft. You're just saying that because you're my best friend."

"Absolutely," I say deadpan. "You really suck at your job, and I'm just being supportive by lying to you."

"Bitch."

"Love you, too. And, James? Congratulations."

"Thanks." I can practically hear the grin in her voice. "Okay, I should let you prep. When's your interview, anyway?"

"I'm in the car on my way there right now."

"Oh, shit. I didn't mean to interrupt you. Good luck. Are you pumped up? 'Cause I can pump you up. I mean, come on. High school valedictorian. Double major in electrical engineering and computer science. Four-time recipient of the Stark International Science Fellowship. CEO of Fairchild Development. Designer and engineer of over two dozen web and mobile apps. Amateur photographer, superior poker player, and all around awesome best friend." She's rattled all of that off at the speed of light, and now she draws a deep breath. "Whew! Did I miss anything?"

I can barely talk, I'm laughing so hard. "You freak. Do you have my resume in front of you?"

"Don't be silly." Her voice takes on an unnaturally high pitch, and I assume she's still teasing me. "Why would I have your resume in front of me? You're my BFF," she says, now sounding much more normal. "Of course, I know your resume. I sleep with it by my bedside and pay homage to it every time I remember how much better your college grades were than mine."

"I love you, James."

"Back at you, Nicholas. Good luck, okay?"

"Thanks." I frown, still thinking of that odd tone in her voice. "And, James?

"Yeah?"

"You're sure there's nothing else?"

"Not a thing. Why? Have you got something else?"

I press a hand to my belly. *A lot*, I think. But nothing I'm willing to tell her over the phone.

8

After two hours of interviews and meetings, I'm exhausted but euphoric. Exhausted, because I'm pretty sure that I've now met every single person who works at Greystone-Branch, from the mailroom all the way up. Euphoric, because I know from Damien's own policy that it's only candidates the company is seriously considering who get the full-meal tour. Time is too valuable a commodity to waste precious employee minutes interviewing an unlikely candidate.

In my case, I'm not applying for a job. I'd be an independent contractor. But the nature of the project—the creation of proprietary web and mobile software to link company communications and resources across the globe—will require access to not only the company's network but also the employees. I need to understand how they currently work in order to make sure that I enhance their productivity, not detract from it.

In other words, if I get this contract, I'll be here a lot. In this office. And in Dallas.

The memory of my mother's house distracts me for a moment, and I miss something that Mr. "Please call me John" Greystone is saying.

"I'm sorry? My mind was wandering. I was thinking about the architecture of your website."

"I only asked if you wanted some coffee. I thought we could talk for a few more minutes in my office, and then we'll get you out of here."

"Just water, please."

Mr. Greystone's assistant soon enters with a bottle of water, followed by the Vice President of Operations, Bijan Kamali. We settle in the sitting area, a corner of the large office set up with a small couch, two leather chairs, and a chrome and glass coffee table. The area reminds me of a similar section of Damien's office, and I allow myself to relax a little, letting hope settle in. After all, they've taken a lot of time with me and paid a lot of attention to me. That has to be a good sign, doesn't it?

"I'll be honest with you, Nikki," John says. "Bijan and I are very impressed, as was everyone you spoke with today."

"I'm very glad to hear that." I keep my voice steady, but inside, I'm turning gleeful cartwheels. "I'm impressed, too. You have an incredible operation here. I'd love to play a part in helping you streamline your communications processes." That's not an exaggeration. Working with Greystone-Branch would be a huge opportunity for me. Not only in terms of building my business's reputation, but also for learning how to organize and operate a business. Yes, I have Stark International as a model, but I don't ever anticipate running a business with that many divisions. Greystone-Branch is considerably smaller, and yet still global. As far as corporate structure is concerned, I could learn a lot by working with this team.

John glances toward Bijan, who nods subtly. John clears his throat and smiles at me, but this time the expression seems a little strained. "Frankly, we're down to three candidates, and you're all extremely qualified. At this point, we're looking at additional factors."

"Of course," I say, though inside, my heart is racing. What does he mean by "additional factors"?

"We were hoping you could shine some light on the issue of proximity. We know you live in Los Angeles . . ."

He leaves the question dangling, and I grab onto it eagerly. If this question represents the nature of their concerns, then I'm golden. "As you know, I grew up in Dallas, so coming back frequently is no hardship at all." That, of course, is an exaggeration. But as I'm determined to exorcise the ghosts of my past, if I get this contract I'll totally make that happen.

"Travel isn't a problem either. I'm fortunate to have access to my husband's personal fleet and pilot. I can be in Dallas within a few hours. And travel to other locations is just as easily arranged. Of course, if I get this job, I'll also either buy or rent a condo nearby for the duration of the project."

I don't usually flaunt Damien's money—*our* money as he constantly reminds me—but in this case, I want John and Bijan to understand that my presence at their various locations isn't subject to the timetables of the commercial airlines. And while it would certainly be reasonable for me to ask for reimbursement for travel costs in addition to my contract bid, because of the benefits to Fairchild Development should I land this project, I've already talked with Damien about not doing that simply because it makes my proposal that much more appealing.

"That's excellent to hear. And you know that we're looking at a relatively fast time frame. You'll be working with a team?"

"I will," I say, and I fight to keep my smile from faltering. I'd been hesitating to hire additional help until I found out about this job. Unfortunately, now it sounds as if I need the team in place in order to secure the position. "I'm looking at a team of three, including me." I'm hoping they don't ask for resumes of my two associates. While I've done preliminary interviews and have found a few promising candidates, I haven't yet made offers to any of them.

"And you're confident about the time frame? Your recent news doesn't change anything?"

I frown, confused. "My news?"

He glances again to Bijan, who slides him a manila folder. John opens it, takes out a single sheet of paper, and passes it to me.

It's a printout from a web page, and the moment I see the headline and the photograph, I freeze.

"Oh," I say stupidly when I'm once again capable of forming words. "This is—" I swallow and try again, but words aren't coming. My head is too full of what's on the paper I'm staring at.

The headline is absurd—*Soon a Starkling!*—but the photograph is even worse. It's me, passed out on the lawn of Misty's house, my head in Damien's lap.

Suddenly, my whole body ignites as if embarrassment is a bonfire and it's burning me alive.

But what the hell do I have to be ashamed of? I know enough about photography to know that someone standing across the street took the picture with a long lens. *That* person should be ashamed—being nosy, selling private photographs.

And the only people who know I'm pregnant are Damien and the staff at the clinic. I'm certain Dr. Cray isn't the "unnamed source" identified in the article, but I bet the receptionist who didn't meet my eyes when she passed me a pen to sign out yesterday earned a few extra bucks.

Bitch.

I swallow, draw a breath, and meet John's and Bijan's eyes in turn. "I didn't realize any of this had made the papers."

"So it's true." The two men exchange a glance. "We're concerned that your pregnancy may impact our timetable. Not the quality of the work," he hurries to add. "But I'm sure you understand that we're on a tight schedule. And with a pregnancy, things aren't always certain. You could end up on bed rest."

"I won't end up on bed rest," I insist, but I see him glance down at the paper. At the image of me on the ground. *You hadn't expected to pass out, either,* he seems to be saying. *So how can you possibly know what's to come?*

I stand, though I feel decidedly unsteady, and the fact that I'm so off balance pisses me off. Especially since when I entered this office, I believed I had the job nailed down.

Suddenly, I wish I were applying for actual employment. Then they wouldn't have even been allowed to ask about my pregnancy. But Title VII doesn't apply to me, and if these men want to hire another candidate because my pregnancy lowers their confidence in me, then that's their prerogative.

"Gentlemen," I say, lifting my chin. "You've seen my work. You've reviewed my proposal. I have every confidence that Fairchild Development can get this project in on time, under budget, and with exceptional quality. I look forward to hearing from you."

I nod my head, pick up my satchel, and stride from the office. If nothing else, I want the last goddamn word.

More than that, though, I want to get out of the building before the tears come. Because I can feel them pressing against my eyes, and I jam my finger on the elevator button and hold my breath, praying that neither Bijan nor John follows me out.

Only when I'm safely in the elevator car do I let my body sag and frustration take over. I cry all the way from the thirtieth floor to the lobby, and when I step out, I wipe away my tears, lift my head, and go to meet my driver.

If he can tell that I've been crying, he doesn't show it. Instead, he opens the door for me and says simply, "Back to the hotel, Mrs. Stark?"

"Yes," I say, then immediately contradict myself. "No, actually. There's somewhere I want to go first."

I'm in a funk as the driver maneuvers the Dallas streets, and not just about the possibility of losing this contract. No, that's only one tiny blip on a much larger radar screen.

The truth is that even though I've been front and center in the press ever since I started dating Damien, I still haven't developed the knack of knowing what's going to trigger tabloid interest. And it never once occurred to me that this pregnancy would be news.

Or, not news, but gossip. The kind of gossip that sells magazines, makes the rounds on social media, and has over-eager paparazzi gathering outside my office or trailing my car or lingering near the gate to our Malibu property.

I made the decision to put up with it when I married Damien, and I've become much more adept at handling the press. For the most part, they don't even bother us anymore. We'd been in the spotlight when the news leaked that Damien had paid me a cool million to pose nude for a portrait, of course. And then again when he'd been arrested for murder—and when the charges were dropped.

Later, they'd been in our face yet again when Damien had decided to publicly reveal the history of abuse that his tennis coach had inflicted on him for so many years. That's when Damien turned the tables and used the tabloids' interest in him to drive sympathy toward the Stark Children's Foundation, a nonprofit he set up to help abused and traumatized children through sports and play therapy.

There's been more press since our marriage, too, of course. Certainly, our wedding was big news, as was all the publicity and crises surrounding the Resort at Cortez, the island resort that Jackson designed for Stark Real Estate Development—and the project during which Damien—and the press—first learned that Jackson Steele was Damien Stark's half-brother.

There've been blackmail attempts, too. Assholes who tell us that all we have to do to keep things like racy photos out of the public eye is pay. Damien hasn't—not yet—choosing instead to use his resources to fight back. So far, he's been able to thwart the threats. But one day, he might not be able to.

One day, it might be our child at the center of a blackmail scheme. Our child that the paparazzi constantly follows. Our child who will be constantly watched. Constantly judged. Reviled for coming from money. Accused of being spoiled and out of touch.

And as for Damien and me . . .

Well, our every decision will be scrutinized, all our choices hashed out publicly. And God forbid our child ever does anything foolish, because the tabloids will eat her alive.

I draw a breath, then sigh as I wipe my eyes once again.

The press had shined the spotlight on Damien even before he won the Junior Grand Prix at fifteen. He was too young, too talented, and too good-looking. Perhaps they would have looked away once he retired, but then there was scandal. And after that, money and the empire he built. Every step in Damien's life has drawn scrutiny, and I can't imagine that will stop any time soon.

Damien's wealth is a blessing in so many ways. A concrete manifestation of his incredible talent and intellect. And it's so damned unfair that what should feel like a boon—the ability to provide for a child in every way possible—feels so much like a curse.

My phone pings, signaling an incoming text. I scramble in my leather satchel to grab it, hoping it's Damien, but I can see immediately from the message on the lock screen that it's not—*What makes you think you can handle it?*

I stare at the cold, hard words and my insides twist as bile rises in my throat. I hesitate. My instinct is to just throw the damn thing back into my bag. But I don't. I open the app so I can see who sent it. But the number is blocked, and all I have is the horrible text.

I have no idea who sent it. I've never been particularly precious with my cell number. Mostly, I only give it to friends, but I also frequently use it for after-hours business or pass it along to important contacts.

In other words, it could be anyone. Maybe it's some bitch who resents me for having married Damien. For being pregnant with his child. Or maybe it's one of the potential contractors for the Greystone-Branch job, pissed off after hearing the rumors that I'm one of the final candidates.

Maybe it's Sofia, and she's not as healthy as everyone seems to think.

I don't know, and I don't care.

Except that's a lie. I do care. I care too damn much. And as I fight back tears, the words of the text rattle around in my head, banging up against my own dark thoughts. *You, a mom? You, juggle work and a family? What makes you think you can handle it, Nikki? What makes you think you're even remotely prepared for this? For any of this?*

"Mrs. Stark?"

I jump, so startled by the driver's words that I actually yelp. "What? What is it?"

He's turned around in his seat, facing me, and though he's working hard to keep a professional demeanor, he can't hide the concern on his face. He doesn't comment on my distress, however, and I'm grateful for that kindness. "We've arrived," he says as he gestures to the cemetery outside the car. "If you need me for anything at all, I'll be waiting right here."

I smile in thanks, understanding the depth of his unspoken offer. Then I draw in a breath, grab my satchel, and step out of the car and into the Dallas heat.

The cemetery covers several acres, but I know where I'm going, and I hurry along the stone path through the manicured lawn with an almost desperate determination. I don't know why I'm so compelled to be here; all I know is that right now I need to be near my sister.

I don't realize I'm crying until I finally reach her grave and discover that I can't read her headstone because my tears have blurred my vision. I brutally wipe them away, then collapse onto the damp grass right in front of her tombstone. *Ashley Anne Fairchild, Beloved Daughter.*

I trace my fingertip over the words, a familiar frustration rising in me. I'd wanted the stone to say *Beloved Sister,* too, but my mother had flatly refused, saying it wasn't appropriate. So that even now, after her death, my mother has come between my sister and me.

"I miss you, Ash," I say, as hot tears cut tracks down my cheeks. "I miss you so damn much."

I lean back, trying to control my breathing. "I'm pregnant," I tell her. "Damien and I are going to have a baby. And you should be here, Ash. You should be with me when she's born. You should be here to help me decorate the nursery and pick out maternity clothes for me, and tiny little baby outfits for her." I choke on a sob. "You should be here," I say again, my throat thick with tears.

I turn away from the stone to wipe my tears, as if I don't want her to witness the depth of my misery. And as I do, I see Damien walking between the graves toward me, his stride long and full of purpose. I say nothing. Just sit there, amazed and relieved, until he's just inches away, kneeling on the grass in front of me. I know the driver must have contacted him, but even knowing that, his presence here feels like a miracle.

"You're here," I say.

"Where else would I be?" He brushes my tears away with his thumb. "Do you want to tell me what happened?"

"Yes. No. I don't know." I lean against him so that his chest supports me. His arms around me give me strength, and my eyes on my sister's grave give me purpose. And then, with a sigh, I tell him about what happened at the interview. "It was great," I conclude. "Or it was great until they started asking me about the baby."

"Sweetheart, I'm sorry." He kisses the top of my head, and I shift in his arms and lean back, wanting to see his face as I try to explain all the thoughts and emotions that are crashing around inside of me.

"The thing is, when I left their office, I felt all twisted up. Like I was exactly where Mother wanted me to be." I think about the text message and its suggestion that I'm not capable of handling anything now that I'm pregnant. I haven't told Damien about it yet, partly because I don't want him to worry, but mostly because I simply want to flush it from my mind. But the message is like something my mother would say.

"Barefoot and pregnant," I murmur. "That's all she wanted for me. All she wanted for Ashley, too. No career. Just a husband to pamper, two kids, and a dog. So long as everything is picture-perfect on the outside, to her, the inside doesn't much matter. All Mother cared about was the shine."

"I'm starting to sound like a broken record, but you're not your mother."

"No," I agree fiercely. "I'm damn sure not. And more than that, I really don't care what she thinks."

"But Ashley did."

I keep my eyes on the tombstone as I nod. "I loved her," I whisper. "And I looked up to her. But she let the voice in her head get to her. She didn't have the strength to fight it." I turn back to face him. "I'm going to fight, Damien," I say firmly, putting his hand on my belly. "I'm going to fight for us. For you and me and our little peanut."

"Peanut?" he repeats, obviously amused.

I laugh, realizing this is the first time I've thought of the baby as a real person growing inside me. "Yeah," I say. "Our sweet little peanut."

His tender smile tugs at my heart, and he pulls me close "Baby, I love you."

I sigh, content to lose myself in the comfort of his embrace. "You don't have to worry about me," I murmur against his chest. "Whatever it is you're not telling me, you need to know I can handle it."

I feel his body grow tense, his reaction confirming my suspicions that he hasn't told me everything about Sofia.

"Damien, please."

But all he does is smile gently at me. "There's nothing else, sweetheart. Really."

My stomach twists with disappointment. I know that's not true. And I want to scream at him. Accuse him of being a damn hypocrite, because how can he say I'm strong when he's still going out of his way to protect me? When he won't let me share my strength with him.

But I force it back. *Time*, I think. I just need to give him more time. And I need to get the hell away from this place. "Can we leave today?" I ask. "I want to be home. There are too many ghosts in this town."

"Of course," he says, not quite meeting my eyes. "But there are ghosts everywhere. And we're both going to have to get used to fighting them."

9

I wake to the sound of running water, and roll over, groggy, to Damien's side of the bed. It's cold, and I sit up slowly as my fuzzy mind kicks into gear.

We're in the penthouse apartment at Stark Tower, one of our two main residences. We'd arrived home last night in time for dinner, and though I'd fully intended to help in the kitchen, I'd ended up on the sofa while Damien made us omelets and went over his weekend schedule while his assistant, Rachel, perched on a bar stool.

Damien is a man of many talents, but I think what surprised me the most about him was his prowess in the kitchen, and last night, he managed to turn a simple mushroom and cheese omelet into a gourmet delight.

"I'd be perkier if I could have coffee," I'd griped, but he'd only chuckled and offered me orange juice.

After Rachel left, we'd sprawled on the sofa, my feet in his lap. As old episodes of *Law & Order* played in the background, Damien reviewed notes for his morning meetings, and I worked on my laptop. I'd had every intention of scanning through the work emails that had piled up over the last few days, but I kept getting distracted by pregnancy websites. And why not? Until I have my first full-on doctor's appointment next Monday, I'm all about educating myself. Even so, I managed to cull at least fifty emails—and order a copy of *What to Expect When You're Expecting*.

All in all, it was a wonderful, domestic, comfortable evening at home. The kind of easy-going night with Damien that usually makes me smile, and then hug myself because I feel warm and safe and loved.

The kind of night that usually leads to slow, easy love-making before falling asleep in each other's arms.

Not last night, though. Because sometime between the *law* and *order* parts of the program, I'd passed out completely, the bone-deep fatigue that comes with pregnancy drawing me down like a stone into a deep, dark sea.

I remember Damien's arms holding me, my body tucked against his chest as he gently carried me to bed. I'd snuggled closer, my desire to slip back under warring with my desire for this man. "Make love to me," I'd whispered, my words slurred in exhaustion.

"Sleep, baby," he'd murmured. "I'll find you in your dreams."

I'd curled up with my pillow, satisfied at the time with his answer. Then, it had made perfect sense. I was lost and content in this dreamy netherworld; of course, I would want Damien there with me.

Now, though, I feel as though I've been cheated. I'm awake and alone and what had been a vague desire last night is now a raging, burning need. I want the feel of his hands on me. His mouth crushing against mine. I want him to tear off my thin nightgown and take me hard on the floor.

I crave the feel of his weight upon me as he pounds inside me, taking me higher and higher until I explode in his arms, my orgasm so wild and violent it rips me apart.

I need it—need *him*. And I have no idea if it's because there has never been a moment when I don't want Damien's touch. Or if my hormones are making me so damn horny, I'm going to burst if he doesn't fuck me hard right now.

I don't know, and I don't care. All I know is that he's not beside me. And all I want is Damien.

I toss the sheet aside and get out of bed, then pad barefoot to the bathroom.

The shower stall is probably my favorite feature of the entire apartment. For one thing, it's huge. But it stays warm and steamy because the glass goes all the way up the ceiling. Right now, Damien's inside, but the glass is so fogged that I can only see a vague outline of him.

I stand there for a moment, enjoy the view and letting my imagination fill in the blanks. But I want more than imagination, and so I peel off the nightgown and let it drop onto the floor. I don't usually sleep in one unless there are guests in the house, but I'd been wearing it on the couch last night, and Damien hadn't undressed me when he put me to bed.

Now, I stand naked and watch the shape of him move in the steam. I'd been aroused even before I entered this room, simply from the thought of him. But now, seeing him in this wet heat, my body is on overdrive. My nipples are hard, my sex clenching with need. I want his touch—and I damn well intend to have it.

His back is to me when I open the door, his face in the pounding water. I've let a wash of cool air in, though, and he turns to face me. As he does, I see the heat flare in his eyes. More interesting, though, is the way his cock hardens, the immediacy of his reaction making absolutely clear that Damien has no objections to my joining him here this morning.

He opens his mouth to say something, but I press a finger over his lips, then step closer. He's almost finished his shower, so his body is no longer slick with soap. I consider that a good thing, because as I kiss his chest, he tastes fresh and clean.

I move slowly down, licking his skin, teasing the light

smattering of hair on his chest. I flick my tongue over his nipple and am rewarded by the way he grabs my hair, his body stiffening beneath my hands that are sliding down his body, too, keeping time with the progress of my kisses.

I go lower, dropping to my knees as I reach his navel. His abs are rock hard and the muscles quiver under my lips. I can tell I'm driving him crazy, and he tightens his grip on my hair even as his other hand reaches for the side of the stall to steady himself.

Lower and lower, my lips teasing his skin, tracing that magical line of hair that leads from just below his navel all the way down to his cock. And when I reach it, thick and wet, I draw my tongue along the velvet steel as Damien moans under my ministrations.

With purposeful slowness, I lick around the head, then flick the end of my tongue over the tip, tasting the pre-come. Then I draw him in, and as I do, the hand that Damien has twined in my hair shifts to the back of my head. At first he just holds me steady, but as I suck in long, deep strokes, he groans with satisfaction and longing, and tightens his grip.

Right now, I'm the one in control, but I can feel that control slipping from me. No, not slipping. Damien is grabbing it by grabbing me—by holding tight to my hair and keeping me in place as he fucks my mouth, totally turning the tables on me.

But I don't care. I'm too turned on to care, and as his cock fills my mouth and water pounds down over us, I slip my hand between my legs and touch myself, then whimper softly. I'm slick and swollen and so turned on it's painful, and as I suck my husband's cock, I tease myself, seeking release.

I'm close, too, so close I can feel electricity filling my body like an approaching thunderstorm. I can feel the tension building in Damien, too, and I know the explosion is coming.

Doesn't matter. He pulls back, leaving my mouth open in surprise. Then he pulls me to my feet and turns me around, his hands gliding over my wet skin as he spins me. "Hands on the wall," he demands, and I comply eagerly as his fingers slide over my ass to find my core. And then his cock is there, and he's pounding inside of me, his hands tight on my breasts as he orders me to "finish what you started, baby. Touch yourself. I want to feel you come with me."

I don't hesitate, and as Damien's wet body slaps against mine—as he thrusts deeper and deeper inside me—I tease my clit, feeling the shockwaves gather inside me, readying for an explosion.

And when Damien's body goes rigid—when he thrusts hard that one final time—when he releases completely inside me, that's when I finally go over, my deep cry of satisfaction ringing out in harmony with his as our bodies shake and quiver together from the force of our simultaneous release.

When the shockwaves have faded, he turns me gently in his arms, then rinses me off before shutting off the stream of warm water. He opens the door, and steam curls into the rest of the bathroom.

He leads me out onto the fluffy bathmat, then uses a thick, cotton towel to dry me off.

Only then do I lean my head back, smile, and speak to him for the first time. "Good morning, Mr. Stark."

"Yes," he says, matching my grin. "It is."

"I figured since I can't wake up with coffee, this was the next best thing." I say it with a wink, and he chuckles.

"Happy to be of service, Mrs. Stark."

"I'll keep that in mind."

"I've read that pregnancy hormones make a woman wildly aroused," he adds conversationally. "I thought I should mention that I'm always happy to help with whatever you need. Ice cream. A quickie on your office desk."

"Frozen Thin Mints?" I suggest.

"I think that's the first time I've been displaced by baked

goods. Too bad it's the wrong time of year for Girl Scout cookies. Besides, I thought your favorite guilty pleasure was frozen Milky Ways."

I lift a shoulder. "Who can understand cravings? But don't worry. I won't stop craving you."

He pulls me in for a long, slow kiss, before easing back and studying my face. "Now that, Mrs. Stark, is something I'm very, very glad to hear."

"When should we tell everyone?" I ask once we're dressed and Damien is walking with me toward the foyer. "Part of me wants to wait until Monday after I see my own doctor. But I also want them to hear it from us, and not on social media."

"Most people don't believe what they read online. Even Greystone-Branch asked you. They didn't just assume."

"True. And I think the gossip may be mostly contained. That printout John showed me was from a Dallas gossip site. And Jamie didn't say a word. And she absorbs gossip intravenously."

Damien tugs me to him for a quick kiss. "Then we're probably safe waiting," he says. "Why don't we host a brunch on Sunday— mimosas for them, juice for you. Unless it comes up before, we'll tell everyone then."

"Good. Sunday's good. Before then, and it's like we're stealing Jane's thunder. I want her to have the full princess treatment at the premiere on Friday."

"Sunday it is."

I hesitate. "Should we wait to tell Jackson and Syl, though? I mean, he's your brother."

"And he'll understand if we wait. Baby, everyone will understand."

He's right. None of our friends or family will feel slighted by us choosing how we want to share our news. I just hope they hear it from us first.

"All right," I say. "Sunday." I press the button for our private elevator, and it opens immediately. I step on, surprised when Damien follows me into the car. I'd expected him to walk through the corridor to his penthouse office suite.

"Do you have outside meetings?"

He flips the switch to lock the doors open. "I just wanted to say a proper goodbye to my wife," he says, then draws me close for a kiss so full of heat and desire I think it's going to take me the entire descent to recover.

"Mmm," I say when he breaks the kiss. "I have a phone conference at ten. I could text Marge and tell her I'm not coming in by nine, after all. I'm sure she'll be fine with putting off reviewing everything on my calendar for this week." Marge is the receptionist for the entire floor of office suites, but I also recently hired her as my part-time assistant.

"Tempting," he says, then brushes his lips over my ear. "But I'd hate to throw Marge off her game. I'll see you tonight," he says, "and we'll finish what we started in the shower."

"I thought we finished just fine," I tease.

"Trust me, sweetheart." His teeth tug gently on my earlobe. "That was just an appetizer."

"Oh." I hold onto the handrail because I suddenly feel a little limp.

"I'll see both of you later," he says as he flips the switch to release the doors.

I laugh and then blow him a kiss as the doors slide closed. And the last thing I see before he disappears completely is a smug smile filled with the promise of things to come.

Honestly, I can hardly wait.

I'm still smiling as the elevator doors slide open in the lobby.

Normally, I'd just take the elevator all the way to the parking garage, but I'd started to feel nauseous during the descent, and I thought maybe a muffin would stave off morning sickness. So I head toward Java B's, the little coffee shop in the Stark Tower lobby.

Unfortunately, the line is at least a mile long, but since it's a gorgeous summer morning, I opt to go outside to the cafe's outdoor kiosk. I head that way, calling out a quick good morning to Joe at the security desk as I head toward the revolving door. "Welcome back, Mrs. Stark," he says.

"Thanks, Joe." I'm about to ask if he'd like me to grab him a coffee, but I end up choking on the words. Because right there on the other side of the glass I see the familiar dark hair, trim figure, and sharp cheekbones of a woman who so closely resembles Audrey Hepburn that she often turns heads on the street.

Giselle Reynard.

Immediately, my stomach lurches, and I'm suddenly glad I haven't eaten that muffin.

What the hell is she doing here? And not just in Los Angeles, but at Stark Tower?

Damien had sent her very firmly away before he and I were even married. The bitch had not only told the press that Damien had paid a million dollars for a nude portrait of me, but she'd also floated bullshit stories to the media, including the ridiculous rumor that Damien, Jamie, and I were having a three-way. She'd been in the middle of a divorce, desperate and hurting for money, but as far as I'm concerned, what she did was unforgivable.

Damien had bought out her art galleries and agreed not to sue her for defamation if she got the hell out of Los Angeles and didn't look back. The last I heard, she was in Florida.

Apparently, she decided to tempt fate by returning.

I don't realize that I've stopped dead until the mechanical voice of the revolving door chides me to *"Please keep moving"*.

I take a step forward, then another. I'm actually considering just making the full circle back to the lobby when Giselle looks up, sees me, and flashes a tentative smile.

Well, fuck.

I step out of the safety of the door and into the bustle of a city coming to life. People scurrying into the building. Horns blaring. A news helicopter overhead.

And Giselle, hurrying over to meet me, her smile just a little too bright. "Nikki," she says. "Congratulations."

"Excuse me?" My voice is cold. Hard.

She swallows, her smile faltering. "I heard that you're pregnant," she says, dashing my hopes that the gossip was localized in Dallas. "Or is that just a rumor?"

I raise a brow. "A rumor? Who would be vile enough to start rumors about me? Especially about something personal."

Her shoulders sag. "Do you want me to say I'm sorry again? I am. I was a mess back then. I had so many debts, and I was so scared that everything was going to come crashing down around my shoulders." Her mouth twists ironically. "And then it all did crash, and I survived. And I realized that now I have to live with every horrible thing I did during those dark days. So if you hate me, that's okay. I deserve it."

I exhale slowly. "I don't hate you, Giselle. I did," I admit. "But now you're not even on my radar."

My words are biting, and I expect to see the force of them cut through her. Instead, she just nods as if she understands completely. Hell, maybe she does. Maybe she really is contrite.

I don't know.

Honestly, I don't much care. All I know is that she went out of her way to hurt not just me but also my relationship with Damien. And not even out of spite or jealousy, but simply to push her own self-interests.

Even if she is in a better place now, that doesn't mean I'm ready to forgive.

"Why are you here, Giselle?" I demand.

"I have an appointment. With Damien."

"You set up an appointment with Damien?" I can't believe he didn't tell me he was going to meet with Giselle.

"Not with him. Through his assistant."

I nod, relieved. Rachel was only working weekends when I was dating Damien. Odds are she doesn't even remember the drama that Giselle caused back then.

She glances at her watch. "I should go. She squeezed me in at eight-thirty. I told her I was only in town for the morning and, well, I don't want to be late." The corner of her mouth quirks up. "I have a feeling Damien will be as enthusiastic about seeing me as you are." Her voice is high and self-depre-cating. "And I don't need to add fuel to an already unpleasant fire by being late. But, seriously," she adds, her tone shifting toward sincere, "congratulations. I'm happy for both of you. Truly."

With a final apologetic smile, she scurries inside. I stand there for a minute, trying to recall why I'd come onto the plaza in the first place. *Muffin,* I remember and take a step toward the kiosk.

"A latte, Mrs. Stark?" the barista asks, but I shake my head. Right now, the idea of food sitting heavy in my stomach sounds like the most horrible thing ever.

"No," I say. "Never mind, I'm good."

But I'm not good, and that bothers me. Because I can't deny that seeing Giselle has cast a gray pallor over an otherwise beautiful day.

10

What have you ever earned on your own?

The vile words flash at me from my cell phone as I enter my office building. Another anonymous message. Another stab to my gut.

I'd ultimately decided that the first message in Dallas was from another applicant for the Greystone-Branch position. Maybe someone trying to psych me out. Someone who didn't realize I'd already finished the interview. I'd pushed it out of my mind, and since there'd been no repeat, I'd forgotten to mention it to Damien. Maybe I would have remembered if I weren't pregnant, in a public spotlight, and crying at my sister's grave, but all of that drama pushed one vile text message right out of my head.

Now, it's back, front and center and with traveling companions.

And I know that I need to tell Damien.

I'm about to call him, but then I remember that he had to face Giselle this morning. Considering the negative impact she'd had on my mood, I expect that Damien will be equally put out. And hearing that I have a new pen pal isn't going to make him happy either.

I slip my phone back into my bag and make a mental note to tell him tonight.

I'm already reconsidering if I should call him now when the elevator stops at my floor, and I step off, ready to toss a smile to Marge. But instead of Marge at the reception desk, I see a tiny little girl with big blue eyes and coal-black hair. She sits up straighter when she sees me, picks up a pencil, and says very clearly, "May I help you?"

"Why, yes," I say. "I'm looking for Nikki Stark. I have an appointment with her."

From the corner of my eye, I see my sister-in-law, Sylvia, fighting a grin from where she's sitting on the reception room sofa holding the baby, Jeffery, in her lap.

Ronnie giggles, then sighs. "No, no, Aunt Nikki. That's wrong. You can't be *looking* for yourself."

I let my eyes go wide. "You're right! How did you get to be so smart, anyway?"

She slides off the chair and trots around the desk toward me, then shrugs. "I just am."

"You just are?" I repeat. "You just are?" I raise my voice to a tease, and at the same time rush forward to scoop her up, lift her into my arms, and twirl her around.

She squeals with delight. "Faster, Aunt Nikki! Faster!"

But faster isn't in the program today because my ever-present nausea has decided to pay a visit, and so I plunk us both down on the couch beside Syl. Ronnie immediately scrambles out of my lap and goes back to Marge's desk because "I'm supposed to be in charge until she comes back."

I meet Syl's eyes, and see that she's trying not to laugh. "Marge is in Peter's office," she explains, referring to the free-lance graphic artist who has the smallest office suite on this floor. "She asked Ronnie to watch the desk while she gathered some papers to forward to him in Maryland."

"His mother asked him to fly out and help her move," I

comment. "Mine didn't even send a change of address postcard."

Syl frowns. "What?"

I wave away the words, then pull one of my feet up onto the couch. My ankles have been aching all morning. "Never mind. It's not important. I'm much more interested in holding this little guy." I reach for Jeffery as Syl lifts him to his feet, and he toddles over the sofa cushions to plunk down in my lap.

"Ni-Ni!" he says with a big grin, and I pull him in and cuddle him close, then press kisses all over those adorable baby cheeks.

"So why are you here?" I ask.

"Oh. Well. Ronnie has a two-week summer camp in Burbank, and Stella has a doctor's appointment," she adds, referring to her nanny. "I took the morning off to bring Ronnie, and since we were nearby, and . . ." She trails off, her cheeks going pink.

I sit back with sudden understanding, Jeffery snuggled in my arms. I flash a wide smile and then lift a shoulder in a small shrug. "We were going to invite you to brunch on Sunday and tell you then. I didn't want to steal Jane's thunder before the premiere."

Syl looks like she's about to say something, but right then Marge comes back into the room, and Ronnie scurries around the desk to cling to her mom's legs.

"Come on," I say, standing and balancing Jeffery on my hip. "Let's go into my office."

I have a basket of crayons, coloring books, and Lego Duplos that I keep for the kids, and Ronnie immediately races toward it. I put Jeffery down beside her, and when I turn around, Syl engulfs me in a hug.

"Congratulations," she says, giving me a squeeze before she steps back and grins broadly. "I'm so happy for you guys!"

"I'm a terrible sister-in-law," I say, and Syl laughs. "We should have called you and Jackson first thing."

"You're fine. I'm just nosy."

I laugh as she settles into one of my guest chairs.

"Nosy," she repeats, "and maybe a little concerned." She wrinkles her nose apologetically, but I get where she's coming from. Syl's mother isn't quite the nightmare mine is, but it's fair to say that we've both had our share of parental issues. She doesn't know all the details about my life growing up, but she was in the thick of it when I was planning my wedding. So she knows enough to understand that I have issues with my mom—and to know that the idea of being a parent myself would make me nervous.

"Thanks," I say sincerely. "But I'm fine. Truly," I add when she just watches me, her expression suggesting she's assessing my veracity. "I was freaked at first—this was entirely unexpected—but now I'm kind of floating."

Sylvia's smile lights up the room. "I know what you mean, both of mine were unexpected, though in entirely different ways."

I laugh. Ronnie is Jackson's biological daughter, and when Sylvia and Jackson first got together, Syl had no idea the little girl existed. As for Jeffery, he and my little peanut have conception-by-failed-birth-control in common.

"I would have called yesterday, but I didn't realize that the news had spread outside of Dallas. Jamie called me before my interview and didn't say a thing, so I just figured the gossip was localized."

I frown, because Jamie's the most tied-in person I know. She's been addicted to social media and the internet for years, but now she's even more obsessive about checking all the gossip sites. She calls it "professional research" and "staying on top of her game".

So surely she would have seen the coverage. After all, the odds of Sylvia noticing and Jamie remaining clueless are slim to none.

So surely she knew. But why the hell didn't she say anything about the baby?

"It's not too widespread," Syl says, interrupting my thoughts. "That's actually why I wasn't sure. I've seen a couple of mentions that you fainted on the lawn of your family home—true?"

I roll my eyes. "Yes and no. It used to be my family home, but apparently my mother has moved on."

Syl opens her mouth, ostensibly to ask me about that, but I just wave the words off, because I'm really not in the mood to even think about that woman.

"They're just covering the fainting?" I ask. "I should have gone online myself, but I didn't have the stomach for it."

"Mostly just that," she says. "But I've seen one or two sites that say you're pregnant. Nothing reliable, though. Jackson said it was probably all bullshit, but I guess I had a feeling. I've seen you go through some pretty rough stuff, you know, and you're really not the fainting type."

I laugh so hard that Ronnie looks up, startled. But Syl is right. Since she was Damien's assistant before he and I got married, she had a bird's-eye view of our tumultuous relationship—and the obsessive, horrible, invasive tabloid coverage we'd been subjected to.

"Oh, hell," she says, glancing at her watch. "I need to get the princess to art class."

Across the room, Ronnie stands up, her hands on her little hips. "Mommeeeee. I'm not a princess! I'm a mermaid!"

"I thought you were a mermaid princess," Syl says, and Ronnie just rolls her eyes. I watch, soaking it all in, and imagining a day when I can tease my own daughter like that. And, yes, wondering if I'll know how. Because God knows, there wasn't ever a whit of humor between my mother and me.

"Toys back in the basket," Syl orders. "Hurry up."

"I can do it," I say.

"Trust me," she says. "Start them early." She reaches down,

gathers up a few crayons, and scoops Jeffery up in a single practiced motion. As soon as he's settled on her hip, she reaches a hand down for Ronnie, who reaches up at the same time to grab hold of her mother's hand. My eyes sting, and I blink back tears. And though I totally blame it on hormones, I can't deny that the simple, easy connection between mother and daughter has my heart twisting with both longing and regret.

"Did you say something about brunch on Sunday?" Syl says as she shuffles her tribe toward the door.

"Absolutely," I say as my phone rings. "A small group. I'll text you the time. You're free?"

"We're totally in," Syl says, then points to my phone. "Get to work and let me know if I should bring anything." She blows me a kiss and disappears out my door.

I grab the phone, expecting it to be the call I set up with a client in Seattle.

Instead, it's Damien.

"Hi, stranger," I say. "I was just going to text you. Syl was just—"

"Nikki," he says, his voice firm enough to cut me off. "I'm so sorry."

"About what?" I say, then, "Oh! Giselle." Seeing Sylvia and the kids had completely wiped her from my mind.

"I had no idea she was back in town, much less that she'd made an appointment to see me."

"I know. She told me she went through Rachel."

"I was on the verge of throwing the bitch out of my office—"

"Did she tell you what she wanted?"

We're talking over each other. Me, trying to sound like it doesn't matter. Him, with latent fury tainting his voice. He's known Giselle for years—they'd even dated for about five minutes before she got married. And he'd been sympathetic when she and Bruce had divorced. After all, she'd lost pretty much everything in their split. But then he'd learned that she was fucking with me—with us—and Damien had put all of his resources to work and essentially run the bitch out of town with her tail between her legs.

I hear him exhale, and it sounds like defeat. "She wants to donate to the silent auction," he says, referring to the fundraiser for the Stark Children's Foundation that is part and parcel of the movie premiere on Friday.

"Oh."

His words surprise me. I'd expected—well, anything else. A request for a loan. To buy back one of her galleries. Simple forgiveness.

Instead, she's turned the tables. Instead of asking for help, she's offering it.

"Oh," I say again. "Well, I guess you should agree."

Damien clears his throat. "I already did."

I start to say *oh* one more time, but force my lips to stay closed. He did exactly what I just told him to do, so it's silly to be annoyed that he did it before asking me.

But silly or not, I am irritated.

Actually, I think I'm downright pissed.

"I didn't realize she'd managed to hang onto any of her pieces that were worth anything." The words come out sounding false. Like I'm making conversation with a stranger in a bar.

"She remarried," Damien explains. "Not only is her husband wealthy, but he knows the parents of one of the kids in the bus."

Immediately, my irritation morphs into something more gentle. "That's horrible. Those poor people." The premiere is for *The Price of Ransom*, the film adaptation of Jane's narrative nonfiction bestseller. It's a story about five third-graders who'd been kidnapped and held for ransom, then almost killed when a rescue attempt went horribly wrong.

The premiere—and all the activities surrounding it—is a

fundraiser for the Stark Children's Foundation, tickets for which start at five hundred dollars and go up to ten times that.

"She and her husband are donating a Glencarrie," he says, referring to an up-and-coming artist whose work has been garnering six figures at various auctions lately. "I told her we'd appreciate the donation, and that they're welcome at the premiere. I'm sorry," he says again, before I can reply. "I should have asked you first."

"No. Of course, it's okay." This time, I really mean it. She apologized, after all. And she's donating a fortune to the foundation. "Besides, there's going to be a huge crowd there. Maybe I won't have to see her again."

Damien chuckles. "I love you."

"That's a good thing, considering I'm having your baby."

"How are you feeling?" I can hear the shift in his tone. Just the mention of the baby has lifted both our moods.

"Good, actually. I feel really good. Syl was just here, though. The word is out. You should call Jackson, and we should start telling our friends."

"Agree. They should hear it from us. We can tell them when we call to invite them over for brunch."

"And brunch will be one big celebration." I glance at the clock. "I need to run. My client's going to call any minute, and then I'm meeting Jamie for lunch. I'm going to try and work late and get caught up, but I may come home early."

"Pregnancy exhaustion?"

"Try hormones," I say. "And the way they're hopping, you can expect me to jump you tonight."

"As I said, I'm always happy to help you with anything you need during your pregnancy."

"Very altruistic of you."

"Later, Mrs. Stark. And I'm looking forward to an evening of therapeutic aerobic activity."

I end the call and flip through my agenda for my notes. I'm

still grinning when the phone chimes to signal an incoming text. I grimace, expecting that it's my client texting to tell me the obvious—that he's running incredibly late.

But when I pull up the phone, it's not my client.

It's not Damien either.

Instead, it's my new text stalker. And the message makes me cringe:

What makes you think you deserve it?

11

I stare at the phone screen, bile churning in my gut. I hate this feeling—weak, exposed—and for one crazed moment, I imagine myself hurling my phone across the room to shatter against the far wall.

I think about the hard plastic pieces, the raw edges as sharp as a knife.

And I think about how I can get this churning, nasty feeling under control. How I can calm myself. Center myself.

How I can use those shards of plastic as a lifeline to drag me back home.

No, no, a thousand times no.

That is *not* what I want. Cut, and whoever is baiting me wins.

Cut, and I'll destroy everything I've accomplished with Damien by my side.

Most of all, if I cut, then what kind of model will I be for my child? I press my free hand over my belly, determined to safeguard this precious baby. This child I hadn't expected but will now do anything to protect.

What makes you think you deserve it?

Once again, that vile message fills my head.

I toss the phone on the desk and put both hands over my baby, then force myself to take deep breaths.

I do deserve it, I think. *I do, I do, I do.*

But deserve what?

The job? My baby? My marriage?

"Oh, shit," I whisper, as the synapses suddenly click into place. *Giselle.* It can't be a coincidence that she showed up right about the time I got the first text. Can it?

I whirl around for my phone. Maybe I've hesitated to tell Damien so far, but I can't wait any longer. Not if it's Giselle behind all of this. Giselle, worming her way into the fundraiser. Into our lives.

But then I think about it, and Sofia seems an equally obvious suspect. Except that she's all the way in the UK. So that probably takes her out of the running.

Either way, I have to let Damien know.

I snatch up the phone, then actually squeal when it rings in my hand.

For a moment, I'm certain that it's her, calling to torment me. To warn me to stay silent. That she has plans for me, and if I'm not careful, she'll spill all of my secrets to the world.

But then I see the caller ID—*Ollie.*

Eagerly, I press the button to answer the call. At the same time, Marge buzzes the intercom.

"Ollie, hang on. Yes, Marge?"

"Your ten o'clock just called to cancel. Apparently, he had some unexpected travel."

"Tell him thanks for letting us know, and ask him to email me his availability."

"No problem."

She hangs up, and I move around my desk to collapse into my chair. It leans all the way back so that I can put my feet up, the kind of thing that would totally mortify my mother, but that I love.

"Listen to you, big shot," Ollie says. "Bossing around the assistant."

"You are such a jerk," I say affectionately. "By the way, I saw your mom. She looks great."

"You did? Where?"

"I was in Dallas. She didn't tell you?"

"I'm trying a fraud case in New York. I'm wasting precious lunch hour prep to call and congratulate you. And to make sure you aren't a little bit weirded out."

I laugh, then put the phone on speaker so that baby Ashley can hear her uncle Ollie's voice. We've had a few rough patches over the years, but at the heart of it, he's still one of my best and oldest friends. And even though it took him a while to come around to Team Damien, I know that he's not only got my back but that he truly understands that my husband does, too. "I appreciate the congrats. And, honestly, it was a shock at first, but now I'm looking forward to every step along the way."

"Pretty fast, though, right? I mean, it's going to be over before you know it."

"Well, yeah." I frown but decide that his odd questions stem from a Y-chromosome kind of place. "But that doesn't mean I don't want to savor the experience. Besides, nine months is almost a year. That doesn't seem fast to me at all."

"Nine? I thought it was a six-month deal."

"Six? What—" I pull my feet off my desk and sit up. "Wait a sec, what are you talking about?"

"Me?" he counters. "What are *you* talking about?"

"The baby," I say with a definite tone of *duh* in my voice.

"Baby?" he asks, and I'm certain I can hear the wheels turning in his head. "You're having a baby?"

"I—yes. Wait. You really didn't know?"

"I had no idea. I told you—I've been buried in this trial. But, Nikki! That's amazing. Congratulations!"

I draw in a breath, only then realizing how nervous I've

been about his reaction. I grew up with Ollie, after all, and no one knows the extent of my family issues better than he does. "Thanks. I'm nervous," I admit. "But mostly, I'm thrilled."

"You're going to do great." His gentle voice belongs to the Ollie of my childhood. The one who was always my champion. The best friend before Damien came along. I feel a little twist in my heart. Everything is fine between us now, but it will never be the same as it was. I don't regret that, but sometimes I miss it.

"And you'll be a wonderful uncle," I say.

"Hell yeah, I will."

I laugh. "So what *did* you call to congratulate me for? There's nothing else going on right now."

"For landing that contract with Greystone-Branch," he says, in a tone of voice that suggests I've lost my mind.

My heart starts pounding, and I roll the chair back away from the desk. "Say that again."

"The job with Greystone-Branch. You'd said you were nervous about it. So I thought I'd call to congratulate you."

"I don't have the job," I say. "I mean, I don't have it yet. And honestly, I'm not sure I'm going to get it. They seemed pretty worried about my ability to get the work done now that I'm pregnant."

"You did get it," Ollie says. "The announcement's in the newsletter they sent out about twenty minutes ago."

"Wait. What?" I dig in my satchel for my iPad only to realize I left it on the counter back at the apartment. Since I haven't yet fired up my computer, I switch over to email while keeping the phone on speaker. Sure enough, there's a newsletter from Greystone-Branch sitting in my inbox.

And three paragraphs in is the announcement of their new software development relationship with the exceptional team at Fairchild Development.

"Holy shit," I say.

"You didn't know?"

"I didn't have a clue. Why wouldn't they call first? And why the hell are you getting the Greystone-Branch newsletter?"

"Can't help you with the first," Ollie says. "But as for the newsletter, I represent one of their competitors, so I subscribed about a year ago."

"Lucky me," I say, but I'm frowning. "Actually, this explains a lot," I say, then tell him about the more-irritating-than-threatening texts I've been getting. "My first instinct was that they were from a competitor. But then this last one came in right before you called, and I started to think it was someone jealous about Damien. Or the baby. Anything but the contract, because why bother when I didn't have the job?"

"But now you're thinking the person saw the newsletter, too."

"Maybe. I hope so." I make a face. "If I'm going to have a text stalker, it would be nice for it to be about my work and not my marriage for once."

Ollie laughs. "You two do tend to make headlines."

Sadly, he's right.

"What does Damien say about the texts?"

"I haven't told him yet," I admit.

"Oh, that's going to go over well."

I roll my eyes. Ollie and Damien may have settled into a friendly truce, but that doesn't mean they're each other's best champions.

In this case, though, Ollie's probably right.

"I'm going to tell him right now," I say. "I was just about to call him when you rang."

"Then I should let you do that," Ollie says. "And I also need to go. I need about ten minutes with my witness before I put her on the stand."

"Break a leg," I say. "By the way, how long are you in New York?"

"Unless we settle, probably at least another week. Then it'll depend on how long the jury's out."

"We'll do drinks when you get back," I say. "Or you'll drink, and I'll look longingly at your scotch."

"Sounds like a plan. Love you."

"Back at you," I say, and when I hang up, I see that I have a voicemail from Bijan. I call him back right away, and he apologizes that their PR department sent the newsletter before he'd spoken with me. I assure him it's not a problem, we schedule a call for Wednesday to go over the specs and set the first round of Dallas meetings, and I manage to control my squeals of joy and delight until after the call ends.

Then, of course, I call Damien—to give him both the good news and the bad.

"He just left the office for a meeting," Rachel says. "But congratulations!"

"Twitter?"

"Instagram, actually. That picture of you on the lawn of your old house. But the caption was good news, and so I asked Damien and—"

"It's all good," I say, cutting her off. "How long do you think he'll be out of the office?"

"He didn't say. I'm not even sure who he's meeting with. He was over in the apartment, and when he came back, he said it had just come up. Do you want me to leave him a message?"

"No, that's okay. I'll send him a text. He'll call me when he gets a chance."

"Sounds good. By the way, what are you wearing to the premiere? I've never been to a red carpet thing before."

"I'm wearing a white dress with black trim on the bodice and a completely unreasonable slit up the thigh. I was excited about it before, but now I'm thrilled. I figure I should take advantage of the occasion since pretty soon I'll be in maternity clothes. But as for you, you can do a gown or a cocktail dress. Either one's appropriate."

"Gown, duh. It's not like I get the chance that often. Besides,

I think Graham Elliott might be there," she adds, referring to the A-lister she actually met once for about seven seconds. "He and Kirstie Ellen Todd broke up, you know, so maybe I have a shot now."

"Maybe you do," I say encouragingly.

"And if not, there's always Lyle Tarpin."

"He'll definitely be there," I say. "He's not only starring in the movie, but he's the incoming celebrity sponsor of the Stark Children's Foundation."

"That man is seriously hot. I mean, there's like lava flowing under that whole innocent Iowa boy vibe he's got going."

I fight a grin. "You think?"

"Definitely. Except I think the nice guy routine is real. I mean, you never hear about who he's dating, and he's only recently started going to red carpet things."

"Maybe he doesn't like the whole Hollywood lifestyle."

"Oh, no. That's not it at all. He loves Hollywood. He just values his privacy." Her tone is almost solemn, and I can picture her shaking her head vehemently, then leaning forward and cupping her hand around the mouthpiece of the phone as she shares some big secret.

I adore Rachel, but she's significantly more fascinated with Hollywood than I am. Which isn't saying much, though now that I live in LA, I try to at least pay enough attention that I can follow Jamie's conversations over drinks.

That thought reminds me that I'm meeting Jamie for lunch and I want to get some actual work done before that. I finish up with Rachel, then text Damien. *Got the job! Call when you can. Want to share that good news and tell you something else, too. XXOO.*

Almost immediately, I get a reply. *Never had a doubt. Soon, Mrs Stark. . .*

I hug my phone close, because *I* sure as hell had doubts. But I truly believe that Damien didn't. Where my career is concerned, he is my most ardent fan.

I text Jamie next, telling her I'll be at Art's Deli on Ventura at noon, which only gives me half an hour to go through all my emails and handle any crises.

Except I'm not in the mood to work. Not at all. And since my office is less than a mile from the restaurant, I decide to walk there and do a little window shopping along the way.

In the grand scheme of things, I haven't lived in Los Angeles all that long. But Ventura Boulevard has changed a lot in my time here. More restaurants, more shops. Jamie's condo is just a few blocks off Ventura, so we came down here all the time to grab a drink or a bite or poke around in the bookstore housed in an old, converted theater.

Now, I'm looking at the street with a different point of view. I see toys in windows. A shop with designer baby clothes. A store with what has to be the Rolls Royce of baby carriages and a crib that is the most precious thing ever.

A darling little onesie with a giraffe catches my eye, and I veer toward that window, thinking that it's a shame that it's way too small for Jeffery. Almost the second the thought enters my head, I realize that I don't have to focus my baby shopping on Jeffery—I have my own baby on the way.

I can shop for Ashley.

And so I do.

In under twenty minutes, I manage to do significant damage to my credit card. Or what I would have considered significant in another life. The amount I just spent is probably less than what Damien has in his pocket at any given moment. That's something that has taken me some getting used to—this constant proximity to money. The fact that I don't actually have to think about how much things cost. Not as a matter of survival, at any rate. I still cringe at the thought of paying jacked-up prices just because the store or the designer is trendy.

But the point is, I can.

Which is why my shopping bag is now filled with a variety

of undoubtedly overpriced baby clothes, all of which are just so darn cute that I couldn't say no. They're also all unisex, because even though I've started calling the baby Ashley, I'm not completely delusional. I'm just hopeful.

"Congratulations again, Mrs. Stark," the clerk says happily. "Come again soon."

"Thanks, I will." I head out of the store, swinging the pretty yellow shopping bag as I hurry toward the crosswalk because, naturally, now I'm running late.

I pull out my phone as I wait for the light to change, just in case Jamie has texted. She hasn't. I glance to make sure the light is still red before I start to scroll through my emails.

And that's when I see the woman on the other side of the road.

Mother?

A nearby man turns sharply toward me. "Excuse me?"

I hadn't realized I'd spoken aloud, but I don't bother to answer. Instead, I step forward off the curb. "Mother!" I say again. "Elizabeth!"

But no one responds. It's just a crush of people on the opposite sidewalk, all hurrying to and fro during the lunch hour.

I curse under my breath and take another step, determined to get across the street. To find her.

But now I don't even see a blond head in the crowd, which is a miracle in a city like LA, and for a moment, I just stand there, defeated.

Until someone screams my name—and I turn toward the voice and see a fast-moving BMW coming right at me.

12

A violent screeching accosts my ears as the smell of burning rubber insults my nose. My upper arm burns from where someone has grabbed it too tightly, and I turn, startled, to face Jamie.

"What the fuck?" she shouts, looking more agitated than I've ever seen her. "Nikki! What the hell are you doing?"

"I—I thought I saw—"

"Come *on*."

She gives my arm a tug, yanking me back onto the sidewalk.

"But I saw my mom again," I say, stupidly. "She was right there."

I point across the street in the general direction we need to be heading.

"Your mom?" she repeats, and I nod.

I watch as a full spectrum of emotions play over her face. Worry. Disbelief. Shock. Fear.

She squints as she looks that direction, then shakes her head. "She's not there, Nik."

"But—"

"And even if she were, that's not exactly a good reason to get pummeled in traffic. You scared the shit out of me."

"I know. I'm sorry." I scared the shit out of me, too. I draw a deep breath and realize that my hand is resting protectively over the baby. "Jamie, I—"

She holds up a hand. "Hold that thought. Come on."

This time when she takes my arm, it's gentler. She leads me across the street in the direction where I saw my mother, then down a block to the deli where we were supposed to meet.

We sit in silence until she's ordered for both of us, then she leans back in the booth, stares right at me, and says, "What the fuck?"

I don't even know where to begin, but I suck in a fortifying breath and dive in. "That wasn't my imagination. I saw her, James. I'm sure of it. She sold her house, and now she's here."

She leans forward, her elbows on the table, then immediately leans back again because the waitress is sliding coffee cups in front of us. I expect her to say something, but instead she adds about a gallon of cream to her coffee, stirs, and then takes a sip. She puts the cup back down, then exhales slowly. "This has the potential to be seriously fucked up."

"No kidding."

"But if she moved here, why not say something to you? Why just keep popping up in the background like some freakish version of *Where's Waldo?*"

"To torment me, obviously."

"Maybe," Jamie says, but she sounds dubious.

"So what's your theory?" I say, leaning back. I want to take a sip of something warm, but I can't do coffee, and I'd been too out of it to change the order to herbal tea.

"Nothing. I don't know. You're probably right. Your mom's freakish enough to think that gaslighting you is a time-honored mother-daughter bonding technique." She isn't looking at me. Instead, she's concentrating on running her finger around the rim of her coffee cup.

"But . . . ?"

Her shoulders rise and fall. "It's just that you're the only one who's seen her." She lifts her head to look at me. "I've been with you twice now, and I didn't see shit."

"That doesn't mean—"

"No, it doesn't. But you've never caught up with her, and she disappears like Santa Claus."

"She sold her house."

"Lots of older women do. Maybe she wanted to live in a garden home and use the money she spent on landscapers to travel to Europe."

"Or Los Angeles," I mutter, but Jamie doesn't hear me. "Okay, fine. She sold her house and me seeing her is just a coincidence. Just my whacky imagination."

"Don't act like that doesn't make sense," she says. "You know it does."

She starts to count out the reasons on her fingers. "First you were putting together that Dallas proposal, so she was on your mind. Now, you know she's moved, so duh. Come on, Nicholas. We both know you've got mommy issues. And that's got to be on overdrive now." She glances at the little yellow shopping bag on the seat beside me, then bites her lower lip. "I mean, doesn't it?"

A sharp stab of guilt cuts through me, and I deflate. "I swear I was going to tell you at lunch—we didn't start telling anyone until today. When did you hear?"

She screws up her mouth. "I saw on social media when you were in Dallas. That's why I called, actually. But then you told me about your mom moving, and I thought I should just wait until you told me about the baby."

"Oh." I frown, feeling like a horrible best friend. "Listen, James," I begin, but at the same moment, she reaches across the table to grab my hands, saying, "God, I'm such a bitch!"

She pulls me into an awkward across-the-booth hug.

"Congratulations," she squeals, then plunks back down into her seat. "Oh, my God, I'm going to be an aunt!"

"So you're not mad at me?"

"Are you kidding? Not even."

I laugh, happy and relieved and contrite all at the same time. "I really am sorry," I say, but she just waves the apology away.

"Oh, please! I should have told you I knew. I was just—doesn't matter. I'm so freaking excited for you." She props her elbows on the table and peers hard at me. "You're excited, too, right?"

There's genuine concern under the question, and it reminds me of just how well she knows me.

"I was freaked at first," I admit. "But I'm over it. Now, I'm excited. Still nervous about—well, everything—but it's a good kind of nervous."

Even as I talk, I realize that I'm more confident than I was yesterday. "Morning sickness isn't my friend," I continue. "But it's part of the experience. And I'm even okay with not drinking coffee," I add, then take a sip of water.

"Oh, shit. I wasn't thinking." She drags my coffee to her side of the table, then adds cream. "I'll just take that temptation away."

"How about you?" I ask. "Are you excited or nervous or both?"

I expect her to bounce in her seat with typical Jamie exuberance, but all she does is stir the coffee. "You mean about the red carpet thing? It's cool. Exciting, you know?"

"Um, yeah. Hugely exciting." The waitress slides the sandwich we're sharing into the middle of the table, and I grab a French fry, then use it to point at her. "What's going on?"

"Oh, hell. It's just that I thought the gig was the start of a promotion. It turns out it was the start of an audition. And I'm already failing, which means that the premiere is going to be my first and last time to walk a red carpet or do celebrity interviews or any of that stuff. And then I'm back to an anchor desk—which is a great job, don't get me wrong, but now that they've dangled the entertainment reporter carrot . . ."

She trails off with a frustrated sigh while I try to filter through everything she's just rattled off and make some sense of it.

"I've already asked Jane and Lyle."

"Asked them?"

"To do an interview with me," she explains.

"They said no?" That doesn't seem like something either one of them would do.

"They said yes. The studio said no. I can catch them on the red carpet to chat about their outfits and how excited they are about the movie, but no one-on-one interview. Apparently, the studio's already set up exclusives with another network."

"So you're telling me that you have to go out and set up your own interviews? That sucks."

"Tell me about it." She looks more morose than I've ever seen her.

"Jackson knows Graham Elliott," I say, referring to another A-lister.

"I thought of that," Jamie confesses. "But he's in Vancouver on a shoot. I thought about asking Bryan," she adds, referring to her ex-boyfriend, Bryan Raine, "but just the thought gave me hives."

"Besides," I say, "you don't want to give that asshole any free publicity."

"True that." She sips her coffee. "We should have done happy hour. I could use a shot of bourbon in this. But I guess you're a no-go on happy hour these days anyway." She sighs. "I'm so fucked."

"The whole thing makes no sense. Do they think you can just pluck celebrities off a tree? And aren't you the talent? Isn't there someone behind the scenes whose job it is to line up the interviews for you?"

"That's the way it works once you land the job. Right now, I think it's all about proving how much I want it. How spunky I am," she adds with a very non-spunky snarl.

"So we just need to find you one juicy story that gets their attention?"

"I think so." She shrugs. "I hope so."

I nod slowly, realizing now why she'd really called when I was in Dallas. And why it had sounded like she had my resume in front of her—because she'd been preparing interview questions.

I reach for another French fry as I consider. Because while I hate the idea of putting the spotlight on Damien and me and the baby, I'm not naive enough to think we can avoid it forever. So maybe it's better to jump right in and take control of the conversation from the get-go?

I draw a breath, then jump into the deep end. "What about me?" I ask as she lifts a section of club sandwich to her mouth. "Or, actually, what about Damien?" Because goodness knows I'm not that interesting. But Damien has been in the public eye for decades.

She drops the sandwich back to the plate, but her mouth stays open.

"James?"

"Are you serious? An interview with you and Damien? If you mean it, that would be amazing."

"I mean it," I say. "And you could have asked when you called me in Dallas."

She sags, looking a bit sheepish. "I thought about it, obviously. But I know how much you hate interviews, and you were freaked about your mom, and—look, Nicholas, are you sure?"

"Totally. I'd rather do an interview with you than have rumors floating around out there."

"And Damien?"

"It'll be fine," I say, and she just nods. We both know that if I ask him, he'll do the interview.

"We'll do it on the red carpet," she says.

"And you'll keep it short?"

"Hey, it's fine by me," she says. "I figure short is one hell of a lot more than any other reporter will get, right?"

I laugh. "Only you, James," I promise. "Only you."

She thrusts her hand across the table. "Pinkie swear," she says. "Best friends forever, and we'll always have each other's backs."

"Always," I agree. "And you'll get the job, James. You're awesome, so how could you not?"

"Speaking of awesome and jobs, what happened at your interview? Any word yet?"

"I got it." Just saying the words makes me giddy all over again. "I found out this morning, actually."

"Ha! That's fabulous! And damn, but we are an awesome pair."

"I'm just hoping I can survive morning sickness, stay awake long enough to finish interviewing possible new employees, and get everything done on time and on budget." I bite my lower lip. "This is a make or break project, James. Am I allowed to say I'm nervous?"

"Welcome to the club," she says. "You're also going to totally nail it. I've got your back. Damien's got your back. Seriously, you're swimming in a sea of well wishes."

"And a few sharks," I say.

Her brow furrows, but before she has the chance to ask what I'm talking about, I open my phone to my messaging app and pass it to her. "I figure they're from somebody who's pissed off I got the job and they didn't. Or pissed that I was even invited to interview, because the first text came before the offer came in."

I watch as Jamie scrolls through the three messages. "Maybe Ryan can trace them?" Jamie's husband is the head of security for Stark International.

"I don't think so," she says. "We were talking about that once when we were watching some really bad action movie. He said it's seriously hard to trace a text message. And odds are good this is coming from a burner phone, too."

"I hate not knowing who it is," I admit.

"Oh, please. I know. It's some dickless wonder who thinks he's all that, and that a gorgeous woman with a rich husband can't have a brain. Fuck him."

I can't help but smile. As far as I'm concerned, Jamie's assessment is dead-on perfect.

"*What makes you think you can handle it?*" she says, quoting the first text. "*It.*" She repeats. "Huh."

"What?" I ask.

She shakes her head. "Probably nothing. It's just that you said the first one came before you got the job. Did it come before you fainted, too?"

I frown. "No, it was after my interview, actually. Why?"

"It's just that the rumors that you were pregnant had started by then. So maybe *it* doesn't mean the job. Maybe *it* means the baby."

"I thought of that." I press my hand over my belly. "And Giselle's here."

"What?" Jamie turns in her seat. "Where?"

"No, in LA. I saw her at the Tower this morning. She had a meeting with Damien."

"No shit? I bet she's got a serious grudge going. What did Damien say? Does he think she sent the messages?"

I pick up a sugar packet and start fiddling with it. "I haven't told him about the messages yet," I admit.

"Have you lost your mind?"

"I know, I know. But I just got these last two today. And as for the first, I figured it was a one-off, and why get Damien all riled up? But with today's texts—well, I was actually about to tell him this morning, but then Ollie called, and then I headed out to meet you, and . . ."

I trail off lamely.

"Not an excuse," she says sagely. "Trust me. Over the last few months, I've learned quite a few things about the marriage code." She leans forward conspiratorially. "Did you know there are actually rules and expectations?"

I feign shock. "No!"

"Yes. It's quite the minefield to navigate."

"I'm sure Ryan is happy to carry you over all the little bumps and incendiary devices."

"My feet barely even touch the ground," she says wistfully.

"You're loving it. I'm so happy for you."

"You know, on the whole, it feels pretty much the same as being single. Except with jewelry," she adds, waggling her left hand and showing off her wedding band.

"Bullshit."

"Hey, we were practically married before. So it was really no big deal to tie the knot officially."

I just smile, because I know how big of a deal it was. Jamie's fear of matrimony almost made her blow the best thing that ever happened to her.

"So where is the man of your house?" I ask. "You were attached at the hip when you first got married. But that was months ago on Valentine's Day." I make a sad face and try not to crack a smile. "Has the bloom worn off?"

"Ha ha. We're both working to prep for the premiere," she says. "Which means I'm here negotiating high-level interviews with techno-savvy socialites— "

I make a face.

"—and he's with his slave driver of a boss, otherwise known as your husband, to talk about tightening up security." She glances over my shoulder toward the window and the view of Ventura Boulevard. "Actually, maybe he's not."

I frown, then turn around to see what she's looking at.

Right there, parked just outside the window, is a shiny red Bugatti Veyron, one of the world's most expensive cars.

And one of my husband's favorite toys.

Within seconds after I notice Damien's car, my phone pings with an incoming text.

Here. Now.

I grimace, then glance at Jamie. "Apparently, I need to go. You'll get the check?"

"Rules," she says. "It's a minefield."

"I'm pretty sure I've tripped a detonator," I say as I remember that my iPad was in the apartment. And that my text messages flash across the lock screen.

"Good luck," she says, then grabs a section from my half of the sandwich.

I give her a wave, then head outside.

Then I draw in a deep breath for courage before I get into the car and stow my shopping bags at my feet.

Sure enough, my iPad is sitting in the passenger seat. It's quiet now, with nothing on the screen. But I scowl at it, anyway. "Traitor," I say.

"On the contrary," Damien says. "I'm considering offering your iPad a job in security. Certainly it's doing a better job keeping me informed about threats to my wife than the lady herself is managing."

"I was going to—"

He holds up a finger, then waves it back and forth, indicating that I need to stay silent.

"But—"

"No."

I press my lips together and lean back in the seat. I know well enough that it's best not to argue. Not yet, anyway.

"Where are we going?" I ask as he pulls into traffic, and though he doesn't say anything, in a few moments, I have my answer. He turns into the parking lot of my office condo, kills the engine, then gestures for me to follow him.

We walk in silence up to my office, and the moment the door closes behind us, he grabs me and pulls me to him, holding me in such a tight embrace, I think I just might suffocate.

"Damien—*Damien*."

He releases me, but before I can say another word, his mouth is on mine, his hands roaming my body, pulling up my skirt, tugging down my panties.

I'm gasping, my contrite guilt at not having told him about the texts disappearing under a wave of pure arousal.

"On the desk," he says, but before I have the chance to move there, he's lifted me up and sat my bare ass on the polished wood. He spreads my legs, drops to his knees, and buries his face between my thighs.

I shudder with the building excitement, then lean back, putting my weight on one hand. I spread my legs even wider as I use my other hand to slide my fingers in his hair and hold his head as he goes down on me, his tongue licking and teasing and turning me on so much that all I can think of is the building explosion.

Then he pulls back, and I whimper with a disappointment that fades as quickly as it came. Because now Damien is standing between my legs, and his fly is open and his cock is out. He holds my ass in one hand and scoots me to the edge, so that his cock is right at my core. And then, with one wild, hard movement, he thrusts deep inside me, fucking me hard, punishing me beautifully.

"Lie back," he orders, and I do, resting my back and shoulders on the desk. He lifts my hips, then tugs me toward him even as he buries himself deeper and deeper inside me. He needs this, I know. Needs to feel that I'm safe and here. Needs to know that no matter how wildly the world around us spins, he still has some measure of control—even if it's only the control of my body, my pleasure. Even if it's only ensuring that he and I are together, always.

And so he takes from me as hard as he gives. It's wild and brutal, and I'm so wet and turned on that I know I will explode any minute.

I reach my hand between my legs, teasing my clit with my fingers and also stroking his cock as he enters me, harder and faster, until finally his body lurches and he bursts inside me, falling on top of me and pinning me down as the final throes of the orgasm rack through his body.

I squirm against him, seeking release as he recovers. "I shouldn't let you come," he murmurs. "More than that, I should spank your ass."

I'm in no position to argue. Instead, I just beg. "Please," I say. "Damien, please."

He slides his hand between us and teases my clit with firm, sure motions that have desire building anew inside me. Higher and higher, until I'm so wound up that when the explosion comes, I open my mouth to scream.

Only a squeak gets out, though, because he captures the sound with a kiss. That's for the best, I think as sanity returns. I hardly need to shock Marge.

We sprawl on my desktop, half naked and sated from this wild, unexpected encounter. Soon, though, Damien gets up, then tugs me to my feet and leads me to the couch.

"Why?" he says, taking a seat beside me and adjusting my clothes. "I saw the message flash on your screen, so I opened your app and saw two others with it. Why the hell didn't you tell me?"

"The first time was in Dallas before I went to see Ashley. I thought it was a one-off, I swear. And then I forgot about it."

"And the others?"

"Both today," I tell him. "I sent you a text, remember? Saying I had something to tell you. This was it."

He rubs his temples. He doesn't look happy, but neither does he look pissed.

"Who?" he asks. "Any ideas?"

"At first I thought it was about the job—which means it could be anyone. A competitor. An employee at Greystone-Branch who doesn't like me." I shrug. "But then I thought Giselle. Or even Sofia. Or," I add, looking down at the floor, "maybe even my mom."

For a moment, he's still and silent. Then he stands and starts to pace. "I can't believe Sofia would do that."

I press my lips together. I can believe a hell of a lot worse about her, but considering she's all the way in the UK, I'm not going to argue.

"And not Giselle. She's newly married to a man who doesn't like controversy and has a hefty bank account. I don't think she'd risk that."

I nod, that seems fair enough. Everything she did before was with an eye to saving her cash flow.

"Your mother," he says slowly. "You really think she moved here?"

"I think I saw her today," I admit. "I've been seeing her around town, remember? Maybe that was her warm-up act for the texts."

"Maybe," he says, though he doesn't sound convinced.

"So what do we do?" I ask, as he reaches down to help me up.

"For now, we wait. And you tell me the instant you get another message."

"I will," I promise. "What else?"

"Now we try and forget about it, at least for a little while."

"Oh." I grin. I like that idea. "Are you heading back to work?"

"Actually, I thought you might want to do some more shopping." He presses a kiss to my forehead. "Unless you already got your fill?"

"Of shopping for the baby? Not even close," I meet his smile with one of my own. "In fact, I found the most darling crib . . ."

13

Damien's already up by the time the sound of the ocean and the soft light of morning teases me awake. I slide out of bed and stretch, wishing that we could stay here all day.

Not possible, though. We both have empires to run.

The thought makes me grin, because it's true. My empire's significantly smaller than his, but it's growing, and if I'm going to keep it chugging along, I need to park myself at my desk and get through some of the initial tasks for Greystone-Branch.

Before that, though, I have one key appointment, and as I look at the clock, I realize that I should probably hurry.

I'd gone to bed naked, and now I pull on a fuzzy robe and tie it around my waist before I head out in search of my husband. I expect to find him in the kitchen, and I'm surprised when I realize that the entire third floor is empty.

The house is ten thousand square feet—large by normal human standards, though small in the world of billionaires—but still plenty big enough for a man to get lost in. When I don't find him at his desk on the mezzanine level, I assume that he's gone all the way down to the first floor to take a swim or work out in the gym.

Unfortunately, I've assumed wrong.

I'm about to give in and call for him through the intercom when I realize that I know exactly where he is. I head back upstairs to the second floor. Early in our marriage, this floor went mostly unused. Once Syl and Jackson got together and their kids came into our lives, however, we'd furnished one of the rooms as a kid-friendly guest room and another as a playroom. There are still two more rooms that have sat empty, filled with random furniture, miscellaneous boxes of mine, and some packed-up files of Damien's.

Now, I find him leaning against the door jamb of one of those unused rooms, just staring in at the mess of boxes and scattered, mismatched pieces of furniture.

"Hey," I say, easing beside him and sliding my hand into his.

"What do you see?" he asks, nodding toward the room's interior.

"Boxes I need to sort through. I think some of those have clothes I'm never going to wear again." I tilt my head to look at him and the wistful expression on his face. "What do you see?"

"The crib we bought yesterday against the far wall," he says, pointing to the spot he's chosen. "It's close enough to the window for the ambient light, but far enough away that the sun won't shine in the baby's eyes." He turns to me. "Can you see it?"

I nod, thinking about the sturdy white crib we'd decided on after looking at every single one on display in the upscale baby furniture store. None of them had been quite right, but then we saw one with a headboard design that had two elephants, their trunks twining into a heart shape, and a line of zoo animals stenciled on the outside. It's absolutely darling, and both Damien and I fell in love with it immediately. It's a special order, but it will be delivered soon.

"It has a mobile hanging over it," I say. "Another zoo theme." I imagine a musical mobile hanging above the crib, tiny giraffes and lions and penguins going around and around above our little girl as she coos and kicks and reaches for the pretty animals.

"And my rocker by the window," I add. It was the only other piece of furniture we bought yesterday. When we'd set out, Damien had said he wanted to spread out the shopping. To take it slow and savor every moment and only buy one piece per trip.

I was all for that plan until afternoon exhaustion snuck up on me, and I ended up sitting in the most amazing rocker in the history of the universe. And then I informed Damien that there was no way I was leaving that store without being absolutely certain that the rocker would soon be mine.

"We need to figure out colors next," I say. "And we need a changing table and a chest of drawers and maybe a rocking horse."

He grins at me. "I don't think we need the rocking horse just yet."

"Okay, then. A giant stuffed bear. In fact, a whole menagerie of stuffed animals who can watch over her at night."

"And a bassinet," he says. "Because she's sleeping in our room at first."

"Definitely," I say, as he starts to lead me away from the room toward the stairs. "And a baby monitor. Audio. Video. And a backup system."

"You read my mind."

We continue describing her room as we walk. What I want stenciled on the walls. Where to install speakers so we can play her soothing music. The colors for her bedding.

"Only about seven more months if Dr. Cray is right," I say.

"We'll know Monday."

I nod. I don't have to ask if he's going with me to the appointment. There's no way he'd miss it. And just that simple reality has me smiling again.

"What?" he asks.

"Just thinking how much I love you."

"Careful, or I might not let you out of the house. And I think you told me you had a full schedule today."

"I do," I admit. "Today and tomorrow. I'm trying to get ahead of the game so that we can enjoy Friday."

"In that case, I suggest a sensual evening of working together in the library," he says. "Two glasses of sparkling fruit juice. A coffee table littered with spreadsheets and computer code."

I laugh. "Sounds like the evening will have all the makings of an epic romance."

"So long as you're with me, then yes," he says, then pulls me close and kisses me hard. "You're seeing Frank this morning?" he asks when he breaks the kiss, referring to my prodigal father. "Do you want me to come with you?"

"Desperately," I admit. "But I think this is one of those things I should do alone."

Frank Dunlop—who used to go by the name Leonard Frank Fairchild—may be my father, but I haven't known him for very long. He left when Ashley was a little girl and I was just a baby, and he recently made a somewhat tumultuous re-entry into my life.

Though it took Damien longer to trust him—and that trust was earned following some intense background checks—my wariness vanished pretty quickly. Possibly faster than was smart, but I'd desperately wanted to believe that Frank had returned only because he wanted to get to know me. And after he explained that he'd left because of my mother, we'd forged a truce that has since grown into a deep friendship. Maybe even love. I'm not sure yet.

All I know now is that he's in our life, and both Damien and I genuinely believe that he's a good man who made a mistake by leaving his children behind when he left his wife.

I take Damien's hand and put it on my abdomen. "I'm still

getting used to him being my dad, you know? But maybe telling him he's going to be a grandfather will make it all seem real."

"Do you want it to?"

His voice is hesitant, and I understand why. Even with all the horrific things my mother has done, I still have moments when I think that maybe, just maybe, we're going to turn a corner and everything will fall into place. She'll feel like a mom, and not like the wicked witch.

I think it—I hope it—and time and again I'm disappointed.

And Damien, I know, is afraid I can't handle more disappointment on the other side of the parental wall.

Honestly, I'm a little scared, too. But I also know that I like Frank, and I respect him. And unlike my mother, he wouldn't intentionally hurt me.

He deserves to know he's going to have a grandchild. More, I think it will matter to him. And I want to know what it's like to share special news with a parent and have them be really, truly happy for me.

I've never had that experience before. And I really hope to have it today.

I left the house before Damien, who's spending the morning working at home. Now I'm sitting in Coop, my convertible Mini Cooper, at a congested intersection on the Pacific Coast Highway when my phone buzzes.

I grab my phone with trepidation, afraid it's going to be a new vile text, then immediately sag with relief, my mood shooting straight back up toward awesome when I see that it's from Damien.

Miss you already. See you tonight. Until then, imagine me, touching you.

I smile the rest of the way to Santa Monica, and I'm still smiling when I step inside the studio that my father shares with Wyatt Royce. My father's a photographer, and when I first met him, he was looking for a studio to sublease. I hooked him up with Wyatt, a photographer and friend who'd been looking for someone to share his massive studio space.

"I'm so glad to see you're looking good," Wyatt says, entering from his private office with a telephoto lens in his hand. With his tousled golden hair, chiseled jaw, and confident air, he looks like he should be the model rather than the photographer. "I saw that you fainted in Dallas," he adds.

"Just the heat," I say, fighting a smile. "And it's always unpleasant to have the tabloids getting in and reporting stuff without your permission."

He cocks his head, obviously considering my words. "Then you're really—"

"Here to see my father," I finish. "I've got some important stuff to tell him."

He grins, and I look away, because I don't want him to see the smug acknowledgement on my face. As I do, I notice that with the exception of the few prints that have been on the walls for as long as I've known Wyatt, every work surface is covered.

A few months ago, he'd told Jamie and me that he was working on a project that he thought would make a big splash, and now I assume these covered walls are part of it. The weird thing is that if he wanted to, Wyatt Royce could make a big splash simply by breathing. He's the grandson of Anika Segel, one of the last living mega-stars from the Golden Age of Hollywood. And his great-grandfather founded one of the studios.

In other words, he comes from Hollywood royalty. All he has to do is snap his fingers to have publicists drooling over him, and yet he's never once played the family card. He doesn't deny them—and as far as I know he has a great relationship with all of them—he just never mentions them.

Instead, he's consistently flown under the radar. He started at the very bottom of the heap as a photographer, then climbed through the ranks by skill and talent alone. I admire him for that, but it's also a bit baffling. Especially in a town like LA.

He'll even be at the premiere on Friday—but that's because the Stark Children's Foundation has hired him to be the official event photographer. Which means he'll be wearing a tux to blend in—not because he's going to be the one in the paparazzi's sights.

I gesture to the draped prints. "So, this is the secret project? Any chance you'll give a hint to a good friend?"

"None at all. I trust you, but I don't want to risk a leak before I'm ready." He looks at me meaningfully. "I'm sure you understand."

"Yeah," I say, putting a hand on my belly. "I do."

I'm smiling as I head to the back of the studio and the stairs that lead to the much smaller area that Frank has sublet.

He's standing over a light board, using a magnifying loop to review strips of negatives. He's in his early sixties, with hair that's gone gray at the temples. He has the ruggedly handsome, weathered face of someone who spends a lot of time outdoors. And when I look straight at him, I can see my own blue eyes looking back at me.

"I thought you shot digitally," I say as I cross the room to look over his shoulder. Photography has been my hobby since high school, and though I love working with film, in this day and age, it's become impractical. I also hate dark rooms—too many memories of my mother locking me in my room at night and disabling the light switch. And while I know Damien would build me the biggest and best darkroom in the history of photography, I do so little behind the camera that it doesn't seem worth asking.

Besides, I've gotten pretty proficient with editing on the computer, and that's fun, too.

"Mostly digital," he says, as he passes me the loop so that I can take a look. "But sometimes you just need to go retro."

I laugh as I bend to look at the lush photos of Santa Monica at night, and even from looking at the negative, I can see that he's captured an aspect of dark and shadows that you simply can't claim with a digital format. "These are wonderful," I say, returning the loop to him. "Are you going to print them?"

"When I get back. I have the trip, remember?" He glances up at me. "That's when I'll shoot digitally. And when my app comes in so handy. I would have come to your office today. I'm the client, remember?"

"True enough. But I wanted to see you here."

Frank is a travel photographer, and so he spends most of his time bouncing around the globe. He recently hired me to design an app by which he could display and sell his work even when he's on the go, and I came today ostensibly to go over some of the tweaks in the programming with him.

"Is something wrong?" He looks at me with a furrowed brow. "I've got a lot of subscribers now—we're not going to have a chunk of downtime while I'm in Europe, are we?"

"The app's fine. Honestly, it doesn't even need any tweaks. I just wanted to talk to you."

"Oh." He stares at the loop in his hand, then puts it down on the table before looking at me. "Are you okay? I heard about you fainting. In Dallas."

I make a face. "On the front lawn of our old house."

"You're sick?"

There's so much concern on his face that I'm certain he hasn't heard any of the other rumors.

"I'm not sick," I assure him as I keep my eyes fixed on his face. "I'm pregnant. You're going to be a grandfather."

At first, his expression is entirely blank, and I'm afraid that I've made a horrible mistake. That he's been fine knowing me—a daughter who's really more of an acquaintance. Someone he can point to and say that he has some connection with, but nobody real. Somebody he can just walk away from again if he feels the urge.

But a grandchild will be different. So small and trusting. So easily hurt.

My breath hitches in my throat. I'd been a baby when he walked away. And it's with a sudden burst of horrible clarity that I realize the risk I've taken opening my heart even a little bit to this man. It's one thing for him to walk away from me, but I don't know that I could survive the pain if he eased his way into my child's life, and then blithely turned his back.

"I—" I'm planning to say that I'm sorry. That I shouldn't have presumed he would care.

That I never should have come at all.

But he cuts me off, and when he speaks, I see that his eyes are glistening. "Nikki—oh, Nikki, that's wonderful. I can't—" His voice breaks and he clears his throat. "I'm very, very happy."

A wild, crazy relief cuts through me, and I realize a tear is trickling down my own cheek. I wipe it away, sniffling a little, but smiling. "Wow. We're kind of a pair, aren't we?"

He chuckles, then pulls me into an awkward hug. For a moment, I'm limp, and with a quick shock, I realize that this is the first time that he's really held me like a daughter. I draw in a breath filled with hope and love, then squeeze him tightly. "Thanks," I whisper.

"For what?"

I lift a shoulder, not really sure myself. "For coming back."

"No," he says. "Thank you for letting me back in."

I sit down on one of the gray, folding chairs, feeling a little wobbly and emotional, then wipe my nose. "I thought I saw Mother yesterday."

It feels like a complete non sequitur, but Frank seems to understand the way my mind works even better than I do, because he cocks his head, pulls a chair close to me, and says, "Do you want to let her back in, too?"

"No."

The word is sharp and fast and firm, but even as I say it, my heart aches. Now that I'm going to be a mom, the absence of my own mother seems doubly painful.

"No," I repeat, this time with less certainty. "But I want to know what she's doing. She left Dallas. I think she came here. I think she's watching me, and I don't know why."

He rubs the side of his mouth with his thumb, something I've noticed that he does when he's about to say something he's not sure I'll like. I first noticed it when he asked me to change the menu configuration on the app. I didn't mind doing it, but apparently he thought I'd be irked that he didn't care for the way I'd laid out all the elements.

"What?" I press, when he stays silent.

"Now, don't take this the wrong way, but maybe you imagined her. Your mother's not exactly the type to hide in the shadows, is she?"

I hesitate, because the times I've seen her she's seemed so real. But he's right—Elizabeth Fairchild is not the kind to hide. "I don't know," I say. "But you might have a point. I'm not keen to think I'm hallucinating, but that's better than having her be real," I tilt my head from side to side. "So thanks. I think."

He chuckles. "That's what fathers are for." As soon as he's said the words, I can see that he wants to take them back. He *is* my father, but we've never really gone there. And in this one conversation, I've had a fatherly hug and this paternal support. Obviously, he's thinking that maybe he's taken it a step too far.

But he hasn't. Just the opposite, in fact. And when I say, "Yeah, that's exactly what dads are for," I hope he understands.

He clears his throat. "So, ah, I know you don't need me right here—you did just fine over the years without me—but I'm wondering if now, well, with you being pregnant and all—" He pauses to take a deep breath. "Well, I was just wondering if I should postpone my trip."

"Oh!" I hadn't even thought of that. He's leaving for Ireland tomorrow morning, and from there, he's going to the

Cotswolds and then Paris and Prague and a bunch of different destinations in Germany and Italy. It's a six-month-long itinerary, and he's not just traveling to shoot stock, he also has some specific gigs lined up.

"No," I say. "You should go. I mean, I want you here, of course, but it's not like anything much is going to happen for a while. And you'll be back before I'm due."

"I don't know . . ."

"I do," I say. "This is your livelihood. I'm not going to stop working. You don't need to either."

His mouth thins and he nods. "All right. If you're sure."

I nod, but part of me isn't sure. Part of me wants him here. Part of me thinks that's what parents do.

And part of me wonders how I can actually be a parent without understanding the nuances at all, having never really experienced them.

"I'm sure," I repeat, and then nod, because I know it's the right decision. "And thanks, Grandpa."

14

I spend the rest of the afternoon tweaking Frank's app because I want it to be fully functional before he leaves the country. Fortunately, I finish it at the office, because by the time I get home and am ready to settle in with Damien, I'm pulled under by exhaustion again. I end up dozing on the couch with my feet on his lap while he alternates between reading science journals and financial reports.

"This is tops of my list," I murmur when I manage to peel open my eyes.

"What's that, baby?"

"Questions for the doctor. This one is at the top. When does it end? I feel like I'm only living half a life."

"Ah, but it's a half with foot massages," he says, putting down his magazine and rubbing my swollen feet and ankles in a way that makes me think I've discovered heaven. "And I looked it up. It gets better after the first trimester."

"I'm not sure this massage can get any better."

"I meant the exhaustion," he says with a laugh.

"How about the swelling in my ankles and feet?" I've

switched to flats, but it's still uncomfortable. "It'll get better after the first trimester, too, right?"

"Actually, it's usually worse later. Apparently, swelling is normal early in a pregnancy, just not common."

"Great." I frown as I prop myself up on my elbows. "You really looked all this up?"

He looks at me like I've just asked the world's silliest question. "Of course I did."

I sigh, feeling satisfied and loved. *Yes*, I think before I drift off. *Of course, he did.*

I wake in bed to the sound of a helicopter landing in our backyard and remember that Damien has a breakfast meeting in San Diego. But he'd told me he would be back by noon if I needed anything.

I can't imagine what that would be since my entire day is going to consist of working on the Greystone-Branch project in my office, something I fully intend to jump into after I eat the pancakes that Damien left warming for me in the oven.

So far, I haven't had pregnancy cravings, but if I do, I hope it's for chocolate chip pancakes, because the ones Damien makes are almost as orgasmic as the man himself.

By the time I get out the door and into Coop, I'm in the kind of good mood that even the pile-up of traffic on PCH can't shatter. I make it to my office with a full hour to spare before my interview with Laura, a recent engineering grad, who I'm seriously hoping is going to be as awesome today as she was when I did the first interview. Because if so, I'm offering her the job.

I keep Laura's resume on my desktop while I start working through my list of action items. I'm on number eight by the time eleven o'clock rolls around, and Laura is officially an hour late.

I skip lunch, just in case she's stuck in traffic and her cell phone is dead.

She doesn't show.

At two, I call her. She answers on the first ring with, "Yeah?"

"Laura? It's Nikki Stark."

"Oh, hey. Hang on." She must be putting her hand over the microphone because I hear a horrible rustling, then her muffled voice. "No, no, that's going to Goodwill. But *that* box needs to go into the truck. Sorry about that," she says, her voice returning to normal.

"You're moving."

"Um, yeah."

"You know we had an interview today."

"Oh, man. I'm really sorry." She doesn't sound sorry. "I'm moving to Silicon Valley, and I need to—*no, no, not that box.*"

"I'll let you go," I say. "Good luck."

"Oh, thank—" she begins, but I've already hung up and tossed the phone on the desk in disgust.

Shit.

I'm reaching for the phone to call my second choice when it starts to ring. It's Frank, and I snatch it up. "Hi. Aren't you on a plane?"

"Delayed. I'm at the gate. What's wrong?"

"Just work stuff." I'm surprised—and a little impressed—that he could tell that I was irritated. It's nice in a weird way. Like he really is a parent. "Why are you calling? Just so I can wish you a good trip again?"

"Your mother called me."

I'd been rising out of my chair—but now I plunk back down. Hard. "Oh."

"You were right. She's in town." He clears his throat. "She—she's rented an apartment. And she wants to see you."

I clutch the edge of the desk so hard the wood cuts into my hand. "I don't want to see her."

"I don't blame you, kiddo. But, ah, I probably shouldn't have, but I told her you were pregnant. She got wind of the story out of Dallas, and I just—"

"It's fine," I say, even though it really isn't. I don't want her to know. It's too intimate a secret. Too special. And I'm too afraid that she'll ruin it. More than that, I'm scared of that tiny part inside of me that—despite everything—wants to hear her congratulations.

"Yeah, well, I'm not so sure. I regret it now, anyway. She said—well, she said it would destroy your figure." The words sound heavy. As if he wishes he could drop them and let them just sink away.

"That sounds like Mother. What else did she say?"

"She wants you to call her."

"I didn't call her after she moved. I don't know why I'd call her now."

"Not arguing. Just passing along the message." He hesitates, then says, "I'm going to cancel the trip."

"The hell you are. You're already at the airport. Your bags are already checked."

"I should be there for you. What if she comes to your office? To your house."

"I have Damien," I say. "Plus, I can take care of myself."

The silence on the other end of the phone is heavy. "I should never have left you. Never left Ashley."

"Stop it. Just stop it." I manage to keep my voice steady even though my insides are churning merely from the thought that my mother is in the same town as I am. "You're here for me now, and that's true even if you are in Europe. You cancel, and it's like you're giving her the power. Trust me, Dad. I spent way too much time shifting my life around because of that woman."

"Dad," he repeats, his voice so soft I almost can't hear him.

With a small shock, I realize it's the first time I've called him that. "Yeah," I say, my voice just as soft. I clear my throat and force a smile into my voice. "So, anyway, I'll see you in a few months, okay. I'll be the one waddling toward you in the airport."

I keep my voice cheery—and I mean what I say—but at the same time, I'm all twisted up inside.

She's here.

She's really here in LA.

As soon as we hang up, I start to dial the phone again—then stop. Because it's not just Damien's voice I want. It's the man.

I glance at the time—already three. I know he'll be back from his lunch appointment, and I also know that even if he's in the middle of a conference call or another meeting, if I ask Rachel to interrupt, he'll come to me.

I hate that I'm even considering interrupting his work. I hate that I'm truly that weak.

But where my mother is concerned, dammit, I am.

And if I'm going to get through this—if I'm going to keep my head and my emotions on straight—I need him.

Dear God, I need him.

I'm not entirely sure how I get to my car, but the next thing I know I'm on the 101 and I'm headed toward downtown. Honestly, my head's in such a mess, I probably should have called a cab or had Edward pick me up. But I make it downtown without causing a horrific accident, and then take our private elevator all the way from the parking structure up to the penthouse on fifty-seven.

I get out of the elevator on the office side, then head straight past the reception desk for the closed door to his office. "Is he alone?"

"He's not here at all," Rachel says. "I'm catching up on paperwork."

"Not here?" I think back, trying to remember what appointment I'd forgotten. "I thought he was coming back after his lunch."

"That was the plan, but some sort of crisis came up and he had to go to Santa Barbara. Is there a problem? Do you want me to call him?"

"I—no." I must look more shaken than I thought if Rachel is offering to call Damien for me. "I just finished work early and thought I'd entice him into the apartment."

She laughs. "He's going to be sorry he missed out on that."

"Well, I'm going over there now. When you see him, tell him I'm waiting." I force a light-hearted wink, and she laughs.

"Will do."

I make a point of seeming nonchalant as I head back to the elevator. Normally, I'd walk down the corridor that connects the office side to the apartment's rear entrance, but that keeps me in Rachel's sight for longer than I think I can handle. And right now, I'm certain my legs are going to collapse out from under me, and I really don't want her to see that.

The elevator has doors on both sides, and I know that it's sitting right there, just waiting for me. I want to scream and cry and rant, but I'm pushing all that down, forcing myself to look normal. To act normal. To give absolutely nothing away to Rachel, whose eyes are burning into my back as I press the elevator call button. The office-side door opens, and I step on, then punch in the code to operate the opposite door that enters the apartment.

It glides soundlessly open, and I step into the familiar foyer, and as soon as the door closes behind me, I quit fighting. A wave of tumultuous emotions crashes over me, and I sink down to the tile with no goal other than trying to control my breathing.

The only ornament in the foyer is a round marble table topped by a stunning flower arrangement that the office staff replaces weekly. The vase is pottery, and as I climb back onto my feet, I imagine myself ripping at those flowers. Pulling them out and strewing them across the floor, the thorns on the roses scraping my skin and raising a thin line of blood. My arms, lashing out to send the vase crashing to the ground. My knees aching as I kneel on the hard marble floor. As I reach for the shards. As I trace the ragged pottery deeper and deeper along the path the rose cut.

As I finally—*finally*—cling to the pain and let it pull me away from thoughts of my mother. From my fears. From all of the anxiety that swirls around inside of me.

My mother.

I don't want her in my head. I don't want to see her.

Most of all, I don't want to lose myself simply because she's near.

What I want is Damien. I want him here. I want him next to me. And I hate that I'm unreasonably irritated that he's not here beside me when I need him.

I swallow, breathing hard, then pull my phone out of my purse.

I start to dial—and then with one violent sob, I hurl the phone across the room, then watch with pleasure as it smashes against the far wall, bits of glass and plastic scattering everywhere.

I gasp, choking on a sob.

I should be stronger than this.

I *am* stronger than this.

But as I crawl to the living room and curl up on the couch, my hand pressed against my abdomen to shield the baby, I know that I'm not.

And as the tears stream down my face, I can't deny that no matter what Damien says, I'm not really strong at all.

15

"Goddammit, Charles, I'm not interested in your best guess. I want some fucking answers. I need to know if she's really—"

Damien's voice stops, and I stay perfectly still on the sofa, my head still fuzzy from sleep. I realize he must have come in through the rear, and now he's passing the archway that leads into the foyer.

The foyer where the shards of my phone are still scattered all over the floor.

"Just get me answers," he says, his voice low and distracted as he ends the call.

I wait, perfectly still, as he whispers, "Nikki," under his breath. Then his footsteps continue, and I realize he hasn't seen me and is heading for the bedroom.

A moment later, he's back. I'm still on the sofa, my arms clutching a pillow and my eyes toward the floor. But even without seeing him, I can tell that he's standing behind me. "Oh, baby," he whispers, then reaches over the couch to brush my shoulder. The touch lasts only a moment, but I soak it in like a tonic, and by the time he's come around the couch to sit beside me, I've propped myself up on the pillow and am reaching for his hand.

"I called you," he says. "I guess now I know why I only got voicemail."

"What time is it?"

"Late," he says. "I came back to pick up a few things, and then I was going to head to Malibu. And to you, I thought. What are you doing here, baby?" The question is simple, his voice steady. It doesn't matter. I hear the worry in his tone. And I hear the unspoken question, too—*What happened, and are you okay?*

I push myself up, my head full of fuzz. "I came to see you, and Rachel said you'd gone." I rub my eyes, grainy with sleep. My head aches, and I know it's the hangover-like effects of a crying jag. "What was in Santa Barbara?"

He waves a dismissive hand. "Just work. Just one of a hundred fires that never seem to go away."

"You didn't text me." Usually, Damien sends me a text whenever he has to head out unexpectedly.

"Sorry about that. I didn't expect to be gone that long, and I had Charles on the phone for most of the flight there. But I did call. You might not have gotten the message, what with your phone being in a million pieces. Nikki," he says, his tone shifting from light to firm as squeezes my hand. "Are you okay? You didn't—"

"*No.*" I cut him off firmly, because that answer is absolutely one hundred percent true. "But I wanted to," I admit, because this is Damien. And because he needs to know.

His body goes tense, and his eyes cloud with worry. "What happened?"

It takes me a second, but I manage to say, "My mother's here. In LA, I mean. Really, positively here." I wanted the words to come out strong so that it at least sounds like I have a handle on this. Instead, my voice is choked. I sound lost. And the moment I see the mix of anger and loathing and regret on Damien's face, my throat fills with tears, and I sit up so that I can cling to him, letting his body shield me from a reality I really don't want to face.

"Baby. Oh, baby, are you sure?"

I nod against his shoulder, damp with my tears. "She called Frank. She wants to see me."

"Fuck that," he says, his voice so harsh that I actually smile.

"Yeah," I say. "I guess."

His brow furrows as he studies my face. "Do you want to see her?"

"No." My answer is firm and automatic and true. But then my shoulders sag as another truth follows. "But I want to know what she wants."

"Nothing good, that's for damn sure."

I draw a breath and sit up straighter because I know he's right. There is no happy reunion scene in the making. No running across a field to hug my mother. No shopping montage. No tender moment where she helps me paint the nursery. I want that, though. Despite everything, I want it.

And the fact that I will never have it weighs heavily on my heart.

"Baby—"

"No." I hold up a hand. "You're right. And I don't want to think about her anymore. I'm done." I plaster on a smile, in the hopes that my actual mood will follow.

"Why don't we go away after the premiere tomorrow?" he asks.

"Really? Just run away?"

He laughs. "Why not? From your mother, from horrible text messages. From everything," he adds firmly.

I should protest. I should point out that I have to work on the Greystone-Branch project because our little peanut is sapping my energy, and I need all the coherent working hours I can gather. I should mention that I need to keep interviewing, and I should spend part of the weekend culling resumes.

I should be responsible and just say no.

But the idea of escaping for a few days sounds too much like heaven. So instead, I nod. "All right," I say. "I'm in. Where should we go?"

"I was thinking the bungalow," he says, referring to our darling vacation home at The Resort at Cortez. It's a Stark Vacation Property that Jackson designed, and it's amazing. It's also accessible only by boat or helicopter, and just the idea of getting there makes me ill.

"Veto," I say. "Maybe after morning sickness passes. Not until."

"Fair enough. The Lake Arrowhead house?"

I'm tempted, but now that Santa Barbara is on my mind, it's too enticing to ignore. "Why don't we go back to the Pearl?"

Stark Real Estate owns the Santa Barbara Pearl Hotel, and we'd stayed there recently for Damien's birthday. But that had been a whirlwind trip. "I feel like we only got an appetizer on your birthday," I continue. "Now it's time for the main course."

"A nice thought," he says. "But let's put that off for a while."

I lean back to see him better. He hasn't said anything specific, but I know this man too well. His expressions. His tones. His posture.

"Did something happen there today?"

"What could have happened?" he asks, which isn't an answer at all.

"What's going on?" I ask, because now my curiosity is roused. "What was today's trip about?"

"I told you. Just some business with Charles."

"And you don't want to go to Santa Barbara because . . . ?"

He stands up. "Dammit, Nikki, why don't you want to go to Lake Arrowhead?"

"*No.*" I stand up, too, my hands on my hips as I stare him down. I'm not sure if my certainty that he's holding something back is real and rational and based on the fact that I know him so well, or if it's some sort of pregnancy-induced psychosis. All I know is that, in that moment, I am absolutely, one hundred percent convinced that he is keeping something from me.

"Do not try to turn this around on me," I say, my voice rising. "Tell me what the hell is going on."

"Nothing," he says in a calmly infuriating way. "There's nothing going on."

"Bullshit." I slam my hands up against his chest and give him a light shove. "Do you think I'm blind? Deaf? That I can't see your face and hear the tone of your voice. I love you, remember? And I know you think you're protecting me. But dammit, you're not. All you're doing is pissing me off."

"Nikki . . ." His voice is tight with emotion.

"You say I'm strong, but then you build these walls to protect me."

"No—"

"And you're so busy protecting me that you aren't even here for me." The words burst out, the anger behind them surprising me as much as Damien. "I came back here needing you, Damien. And you were off chasing some secret bullshit that you won't even tell me about? No—I'm sorry, but *no.*"

I draw a breath. "We promised each other no secrets—and over and over again you've told me that I'm strong enough to handle all the shit that keeps getting piled on us. Was that all smoke and mirrors?"

"You know it wasn't."

"Is it the baby? Do you see me differently now?"

"Not differently," he says, stepping closer, so that I have to back up to keep some distance. "More."

He's right in front of me, so close I can feel the energy buzzing off him. "You're the mother of my child, Nikki."

"And that makes me weak? That gives you the right to keep secrets from me?"

"No—God, Nikki, no." He starts to run his fingers through

his hair, but stops and reaches for me instead, looking more lost than I've ever seen him. I lean toward him, wanting so desperately to fall into his arms. But I know what will happen. I'll lose myself in his touch. I'll drown in his embrace. And I'll forget my fears and my anger and my worries because the bottom line is that I do know that he loves me.

But I don't want to forget. I don't want to be coddled.

So I shake my head and lift my chin. I look at him through tear-filled eyes. "You made me a promise once, Damien. No more secrets." I press my hands protectively over my belly. "And no matter what you think, this shouldn't change that."

I wipe tears away as I rush to the bedroom, expecting him to follow. He doesn't, though, and my insides twist even more, this time with fear. There's a gulf between us right now. A gaping chasm filled with uncertainty and secrets, and it's one that I don't know how to cross. I don't even know where it came from.

Except I do. And as I press my hand over the baby, my tears start to flow in earnest, because how the hell can we manage as parents if we can't even manage a pregnancy?

It's a horrible, terrifying thought, and the weight of it pulls me under as I lie there for I don't know how long, listening to Damien pacing in the other room, then his footsteps coming closer and closer.

He pauses in the doorway. "Nikki?" His voice is soft. "Sweetheart?"

I keep my eyes closed and my breathing steady. I'm tempted to lift my head and roll over so that I can see him, but I'm lost in that space between sleep and wakefulness. And the truth is that I don't want to emerge from it. Not yet. Not even for Damien. And so I keep my eyes closed and my breathing steady.

After a moment, I hear his footsteps again, this time coming closer. I wait for him to kiss me or rub his hand over my arm, anything to gently wake me. But instead, he simply takes the folded blanket from the foot of the bed and pulls it over me. Then he runs a soft hand over my hair before turning back toward the door.

For the briefest moment, I consider calling him back. But then the lights go off and the door snicks softly closed, and I'm left alone in the dark with my thoughts and my fears.

16

I'm still on top of the bedspread and under the thin blanket when I wake in the morning. Damien isn't beside me, and a horrible loneliness washes over me. Except when one of us is traveling, we've always slept together. And I hate that it's secrets and lies pushing us apart now. Especially since we'd fought so hard to shine a light on the gray areas between us before we'd walked down the aisle.

I push the blanket away and sit up, and only then do I notice the dent in the pillow beside me and the afghan crumpled at the foot of the bed. I close my eyes, fighting tears that I tell myself are from a morning rush of hormones, but that I know very well are tears of relief.

As I pad into the kitchen, wishing for coffee, I remember that Damien mentioned an early-morning teleconference this week. That explains why he's gone when it's not even seven yet.

He's left bagels out for me, but that doesn't sound good at all. I open the refrigerator and stare inside, as if some amazing gourmet breakfast will fly off the shelves and onto a plate. When that miracle doesn't happen, I open the freezer with the hope of finding frozen waffles, then gasp with delight at the bags of Milky Ways and boxes of Thin Mints that confront me.

I grab a Milky Way and sigh with pleasure. I really do love that man.

I've peeled the wrapper back and am half-gnawing and half-sucking on the candy bar as I step out of the kitchen to see if Damien left the paper for me on the coffee table.

But it's not the paper that I find, it's the man himself. He's sitting on the sofa in sweatpants and a ratty white T-shirt. And perched on his lap, eating cheese puffs from a purple bowl, is our nephew, Jeffery.

And in that moment, it's as if the entire world has turned inside out. Before, I had no trouble believing the theory that Damien could be a dad. Now, though, I see it in practice. And I press my fingertips to my lips to stave off a fresh wave of tears.

Damien hasn't noticed me yet—his head is down, and there are papers scattered on the couch beside him. He's holding one sheet in his hand and talking in a low voice, as if he's running down a list of project specs for Jeffery.

As for the kiddo, he's clearly having a blast. His mouth is bright orange, and his fingers are, too. He keeps saying "re-re"— which is Jeffery-speak for "read"—and grabbing for the paper with his orange-stained fingers.

Damien manages to keep the sheet away from him—at least until he looks up, sees me, and goes still. Which, of course, is when Jeffery grabs the paper and starts to chew on it.

"Nikki," Damien says, deftly rescuing the slightly stained corporate document. "Good morning."

"To you, too." I move into the room and sit on the opposite end of the couch, so as not to crumple the papers. "Looks like we have company this morning," I add, waving at Jeffery, who grins back at me and shouts, "Ni-Ni!"

"Stella has a doctor's appointment," Damien explains, referring to Jeffery's nanny. "Syl brought the baby to work with her, but then she had a crisis come up on a project in Glendale that she has to handle before you three head out."

"And there was no one else in the whole of Stark International who could watch this little guy," I tease.

"I might have specifically requested the job," he admits. "Get in a little practice on someone else's kid."

"I understand that," I say, switching to a baby voice and bending over to play peek-a-boo, which makes Jeffery giggle. After a second, I glance back up at Damien. "Did you say three? There are four of us going to the spa."

Tonight's the premiere for *The Price of Ransom,* and Sylvia, Jane, Jamie, and I are all going to the spa for hair, makeup, and mani-pedis.

"According to Syl, Jamie's being prepped and primped at the studio, and then being whisked to the theater in a network news van."

"Of course, she is," I say, and though I'm disappointed about missing Jamie today, I'm excited for her. "We're giving her an exclusive," I tell Damien. "I forgot to tell you."

"Courting the press are we?" he teases, and I roll my eyes.

"Yeah, that's me. Anything to get into the tabloids."

One of the promotional flyers for tonight's premiere and fundraiser is open on the coffee table, and I reach for it. The Stark Children's Foundation is sponsoring the screening and the red carpet pre-party, which includes cocktail and food stations, photo booths, and a silent auction. All of the proceeds go to fund the foundation's scholarships.

"It's going to be a great event," I say, looking at the flyer and the sweet faces of some of the younger kids the foundation has helped. I know how much the organization means to Damien—how much he both gave up and gained when he went public with his own history of abuse. Now, I trace my fingertip over the face of a little girl with inquisitive green eyes, and the thought that anyone ever hurt this poor child makes me sick.

I rest my hands protectively over my belly and then turn to Damien, only to find him already looking at me. "I'm sorry about last night," I say, even as he says the exact same thing.

We both laugh, and though I wait for him to tell me what he's been hiding, the words don't come. My disappointment must show on my face because he stands up, Jeffery propped on his hip. He moves to sit on the table in front of me, then leans forward and tilts my head up for a kiss.

"Don't stop trusting me, Nikki. Everything I am. Everything I do, it's with you in mind. With *us* in mind." He puts his hand over mine. "There is no moment when I'm not thinking of you, and I would destroy myself before I'd risk hurting you."

"I know," I say. "I do. But trust isn't a panacea any more than it's a curtain to hide behind."

"It's not, you're right. But I'm not trying to hide things from you—I swear. I just need time."

I reach for Jeffery, who's starting to fuss, then bounce him on my knee. "Time for what?" I demand. "What is this about? I mean, are you—*oh*." I hug Jeffery closer. "This is about the text messages."

I lean back against the couch with a heavy sigh. I should have realized last night. Of course, he was out chasing answers.

"You should have just told me," I say. "What have you learned? Who is it? Is it my mother?"

"I don't know. I thought—" He cuts himself off with a shake of his head. "I don't know yet." He leans forward, one hand on my knee and the other on my cheek. "I'm going to find out, though. I promise you that."

I draw a deep breath, then nod. "Last night was horrible," I say. "I don't like it when there's a chasm between us."

"Neither do I, baby. But there's always a bridge."

"You're remarkably calm for someone with a movie opening in just a few hours," I say to Jane, who's sitting between Sylvia and me. Our feet are in the warm, swirling water, our heads are wrapped in towels to cover the conditioning goop, and we're each about to get our pedicures.

"It's all an act," she says with a smile that shows off her incredible cheekbones. "Actually, I think it just hasn't set in. I've been living the book and the script for so long, that I can't believe it's finally, really a movie." Her brown eyes shine as she smiles, and she brushes a lock of dark hair off her face. "It's pretty amazing, though, isn't it?"

"Are you kidding?" Syl asks. "It's incredible." She reaches over and squeezes Jane's hand. "I'm so thrilled for you."

I've become pretty good friends with Jane, but Syl knows her much better because Jane's husband, Dallas, is one of the investors in The Resort at Cortez. Both Jane and Dallas both come from old money, and I think it's fair to say that they've had the most unconventional and controversial relationship I've ever heard of. It certainly garnered more press coverage than me, Damien, Jackson, and Sylvia combined.

But as far as I can tell, Jane and Dallas are blissfully happy. So I guess it was worth all the drama.

"I'm bummed Jamie's not here," Jane says, glancing in my direction. "And I'm especially sorry that neither Lyle nor I can do an interview with her. The studio paid us both well, but the paycheck comes with a variety of brightly colored leashes."

"She understands, I promise."

"But you can make it up to us by giving Nikki and I a mini-interview right now," Syl says.

"What? About me?"

Sylvia makes a dismissive motion. "Oh, please. What's there to talk about with you?"

Jane laughs, because, of course, there's a hell of a lot. And all of it juicy.

"No," Syl continues. "Tell us about Lyle. He plays everything so close to the vest. Even Nikki hasn't really gotten to know him." She glances at me. "And you and Damien have had dinner or drinks with him dozens of times for foundation business, right?"

I nod. Lyle is the current celebrity sponsor for the Stark Children's Foundation, and Syl is right—I like him a lot. But I don't really know him.

"Honestly, I doubt I know him much better than you guys do," Jane says. "I mean, I wasn't on the set that much. But the times we did hang out, he seemed to live up to his press."

"You mean the generally accepted belief that he's the nicest guy in Hollywood?" Syl asks.

"Pretty much," Jane says, but there's a reticence to her words.

"But?" I press, even as I think that I've been hanging out with Jamie for far too long, because celebrity gossip was never my thing. And yet, here I am, a walking stereotype of a pampered LA woman gossiping in the spa.

"*But*," Jane concedes, "there's something under all that nice. I don't know what. It's just—you guys know about my childhood, right?"

I look at Syl, and we both nod. It had come out publicly not long before their wedding that Jane and Dallas were both kidnapped as children. Which means that my childhood drama with my mother is nothing by comparison.

"Yeah, well, the end result is that I'm not big on the whole trust thing," Jane says. "You never know what's inside people. What kind of monster might be hiding under their skin."

"You don't trust Lyle?" I ask, genuinely surprised.

"No, no. Lyle's great. Really. But I've gotten pretty good at looking deeper."

"And?"

"And there's more to him than meets the eye."

"So he has secrets," Syl says.

Jane nods. "Something that haunts him, I think."

"Something he wants to keep quiet," Syl adds, then sighs as the technician starts to massage her calves. "I can hardly fault him for that."

I think of my own secrets. "Amen," I say.

And then the three of us raise imaginary toasts in honor of Lyle and his secrets. Deep and dark though they might be, they're his own. And I hope that when his star power climbs after this movie—which everyone is saying will be a box office sensation—that his secrets will still be his own.

An hour later, we're all primped and ready. Jane's car has already whisked her away, and Sylvia and I are waiting for our drivers to arrive.

"Well?" she demands.

I blink. "Um?"

"Secrets," she says, in a tone that I'm sure she uses with Ronnie. "I saw the look on your face when we were talking with Jane. What's going on?"

"Nothing," I say.

"You're a terrible liar," she counters.

The truth is, I'm actually a pretty good liar. I've spent my life putting on and taking off a variety of masks. Social Nikki. Student Nikki. Pageant Nikki. And as a result, I'm adept at hiding my feelings.

Which means that Sylvia is either fishing—or I'm actually craving someone to talk to. In this case, there's really no question that it's the latter, and I explain to her my fear that Damien is keeping secrets because he thinks he's protecting me.

The corners of Syl's eyes crinkle as she smiles. "Well, then my advice to you is simple. Deal with it."

I laugh. "Seriously? That's the best you've got?"

She shrugs. "Certainly the simplest. Come on, Nik. He's always going to try to protect you. And now you're pregnant. That means all that protective male DNA is in overdrive. And you and I both know that Stark men got served an extra dose at birth."

I laugh because she's so damn right. "It's still annoying as hell."

"Not arguing," she says. "But it's sweet, too."

I have to grudgingly concede the point, although *sweet* and *infuriating* are not so often intertwined.

"Just go with it," she says, obviously reading my expression. "And by the way, you should come over this weekend. The entire spare closet is full of things that Jeffery's outgrown or doesn't play with anymore. We can dig through it and see what you want."

"Perfect," I say as my car pulls up. "Maybe I'll follow you back to your house after brunch on Sunday."

We plan on that, and I settle into the backseat for the ride from Beverly Hills to Malibu, feeling relaxed and pampered and guilty about having spent an entire day not even thinking about work.

At the very least, I can check my emails. I pull out the new phone that I'd found on the bathroom counter this morning, just casually waiting for me, thanks to my wonderful—and as Sylvia said, wonderfully protective—husband.

Now I open the email app and smile again, because not only did he replace my phone at the speed of light, but he also set up my email accounts.

I switch to the messaging app and send him a quick thank you.

His answer is swift and to the point: *I'd do anything for you.*

I know. I missed you today.

I amuse myself by counting the seconds until he replies. Only seven.

Missed you more. I'm at the house. The limo's coming at 5. How long do you need to get dressed?

I check the time, and it's not yet three.

Not two hours, I type. *If you have some idea of how to fill the time . . .*

His reply makes me smile: *I'm full of ideas. Tell your driver to hurry. And in the meantime, imagine me, touching you.*

I laugh as I send one final message: *I always do.*

I've just re-opened my email app when I notice a new email from *youradoringhusband* at an email server I'm not familiar with. I purse my lips in amusement, wondering what Damien's up to now.

But when I open the email to see what he sent this time, my smile freezes on my face, and the message makes me queasy.

Did you really think you could have both?

Below the words is a picture of Sofia, her head on Damien's shoulder.

And not just one picture, but several. And in each and every one, they're standing right in front of the Santa Barbara Pearl Hotel.

17

By the time I arrive home, my tears have completely destroyed my freshly applied makeup and I'm an angry, hurt, hormonal mess. I order the driver to wait, then hurry to the front door and punch in my key code.

The lock clicks open, and I push the door, anxious to get inside and get my things for the premiere tonight. I'm so hurt and twisted up and hormonal that all I want to do is get out of here. Because I see a huge fight looming, and I can't deal with that right now.

I don't believe the email's suggestion that Damien's cheating on me—honestly, I can't imagine a world in which I could ever believe he cheated on me—but he did keep this huge, hurtful secret from me. And not only did he keep a secret, he actually lied when I asked him why he'd gone to Santa Barbara. He'd lied about Sofia. *Sofia*.

The woman who tried to take Damien. Who tried to destroy me. And, honestly, almost succeeded.

So I need time. To get my thoughts together. To calm my raging hormones. To figure out what I'm going to say to him.

Mostly, to stop this explosion building inside me before I

lash out at him and completely destroy an evening that means so much to so many of my friends.

That's my plan, anyway, but as soon as I enter the house, I'm stopped by the sight before me—hundreds of red and pink rose petals scattered over the floor of the entrance hall and trailing up the massive staircase.

A lump forms in my throat, and though it's hard to believe I have any more tears to shed, when I blink, warm liquid trails down my cheeks. When I draw in a stuttering breath, I taste the salt of my tears. *This* is what I want. Tenderness and love and romance. Not secrets and deceit and lies.

I swallow hard as I cast my gaze around, looking at the romantic setting he's created with the petals and soft candle-light. For a moment, my resolve wavers, and I think that I need to hurry and find him.

But then I remember the pictures on my phone. *Work* problem? I mentally scoff at Damien's explanation of why he'd gone to Santa Barbara. Sofia is a lot of things, but she sure as hell isn't a work problem.

The cloying scent of the roses surrounds me as I crush petals beneath my ballet-style flats in my hurry up the stairs. I wrinkle my nose, fighting nausea, then I force myself to focus on getting my things and getting the hell out of there.

I expect to see Damien on the third floor, which is where we spend most of our time, but he's not there, and I realize that he's probably in the cabana by the pool, waiting with chilled fruit juice for me to find him.

Normally, I'd be tempted.

Today, I'm grateful that I can get in and get out. I'm not ready for a fight—my wounds feel too raw. All I really want to do is find someplace to hide away, curled up into a ball until I can gather the strength to have it out with my husband.

I'd be there right now—locked away in some out of the way motel—if it weren't for tonight's premiere. But there's no way

I'm going to skip Jane's movie or the fundraiser. The foundation is too important to me—too important to all those kids.

So I'll be there. And with any luck, I'll have pulled myself together before I have to step from a limo onto that red carpet.

My closet is huge, approximately the size of the bedroom I used to have in Jamie's condo, and one entire wall is devoted to formal wear. Ironic, considering that once I walked away from the pageant life, I swore that if I never saw another sequin, it would be too soon. But, somehow, dressing up isn't painful when you're on the arm of someone you love, and as I look at my gowns, I feel a little stab in my heart.

I want Damien here—I do.

I'm just not ready to face him yet.

The dress I've selected for tonight hangs at the front, still in protective plastic from the few minor alterations. I use the library style ladder to retrieve my garment bag from a top shelf, then slide the dress inside. I zip it securely and fold the bag over to carry like a soft-sided suitcase. There's a shoe pocket on the outside, and I find the black stiletto sandals I'd picked for the evening and put them inside, then grab my travel cosmetics case, because I'm going to need to do some makeup repair before I'm picture-ready.

Finally, I open the jewelry safe and pull out the platinum and emerald ankle bracelet that Damien bought me when we first started dating. It will be hidden under the dress, but that doesn't matter. I've worn it to every event we've attended together, and I'm not going to stop tonight.

I set it in its box on the granite island in the center of the closet, then consider how best to carry it. I know I'm overthinking—it's not like I'm going to lose it just going to the car and then a motel, but I can't help but be paranoid. The thing probably cost more than Air Force One—and it has a hell of a lot more sentimental value.

Since I'd foolishly left my purse in the car, I decide to tuck it into the outside, zippered pocket on the garment bag. I'm about to do that when I realize I'm not alone. I turn—and there he is.

"What the hell, Nikki?"

He's standing in the closet doorway in khaki shorts and a white henley that accentuates his tan. Over the last couple of years, he's started playing tennis again, and he's all muscle and sinew, the material of the shirt straining against his broad shoulders and strong upper arms.

"I'll see you at the premiere," I say, wishing I didn't want to touch him. "I've arranged for my own limo." That's true enough—on the way home from the spa, I had my driver contact dispatch to make all the arrangements.

His head tilts just slightly, as if I'm a puzzle he can't quite solve. "All right," he says slowly. "Where are you going in the meantime?"

"I don't know." I hook the strap of the garment bag over one shoulder and hold onto my cosmetics case with both hands, squeezing so tightly that I'm certain my knuckles are going to turn white. "A hotel. Sylvia's. I'll figure it out."

I can see only the question in his eyes. Other than that, his expression is like stone, revealing nothing. I have to fight the sudden urge to slap him. I have so many masks that I show to the world, and Damien has always been able to see through all of them. And yet here he stands, revealing nothing, when I'm standing before him, bloody and broken.

"You son-of-a-bitch," I snap, everything just suddenly getting to me. "You goddamn son-of-a-bitch."

"Nikki—"

"*No.*" I hold up a hand to stop him. "Trust you?" I say. "The entire time you were asking me to trust you this morning, you had your finger on a goddamn nuclear trigger."

"What are you talking about?"

"Sofia. You. Santa Barbara. Ring any bells?"

I can see from his face that it's ringing a lot of them.

"Fuck," I say. For a moment, I'd foolishly hoped I was wrong.

I tighten my grip on my case. "Call me when you learn that trust doesn't mean keeping secrets when it's convenient for you, okay? I thought we'd come farther than this, Damien. I thought—"

But I can't finish. I don't even know what I thought. That everything was perfect? That all the bumps that had plagued our early relationship had been smoothed out? That we would be bringing a child into a family without drama and secrets and skeletons hiding in closets.

I don't know. I don't care. I just know that I need to leave, and so I turn and run from him with no real idea of where I'm going or what I'll do when I get there.

I'd meant it when I told Damien I didn't know where I was going. But now that I'm in the back of the car and maneuvering through the twisting Malibu roads as we head down toward the Coast Highway, I figure I need some sort of plan. And since Jamie has always been my first and best go-to in all my relationship-related emergencies, I automatically dial her number.

"Hey!" she says, answering on the first ring. "Guess where I am—in a chair in network makeup. How cool is that?"

"Exceptionally cool," I concede, then bite back a cringe—I'd been so wrapped up in my own drama, I'd actually forgotten that this was Jamie's big day. Obviously, I'm the worst friend ever.

"What's up?" she says.

"Not a thing," I trill. "I just called to wish you good luck."

"Oh, please," she retorts. "Who needs luck when you have all my talent."

I bark out a laugh. "Can't argue with that. Love you, James."

"Back at you, Nicholas. See you on the red carpet."

"Absolutely," I say, then end the call with a sigh. Because now where the hell am I going to go?

I'm about to lean forward to tell the driver we're heading to the Pacific Palisades and Sylvia's house, when I realize there's someplace else I'd rather be. Because the truth is, right now I want a full-on, maternal-style hug. And since no matter how hard I wish otherwise, I'm sure as hell not getting that from my own mother, so I tell the driver to head for Evelyn's Malibu beach house.

Five minutes later, I'm standing on her small front porch, my garment bag in hand, hoping like hell that she's actually home. I'm about to regret not calling first when I hear footsteps and then see her peer out through the peephole.

Immediately, the door opens, and she's standing there in all her effervescent glory, ushering me into the house with, "Well, what the hell, Texas, you always are full of surprises."

She takes my bags from me, then waves the car away before shutting the door behind me. "Let me guess. Trouble in paradise?"

I start to answer, then find myself crying instead. Immediately, she pulls me into a momma bear-style hug, and I cling to her, feeling lost and found and mortified all at the same time.

When I can breathe normally, I back away, then smile wryly. "I shouldn't have bothered with the spa this morning. I'm going to have to completely re-do my makeup."

"Unless you want to go to the premiere looking like a raccoon, I'm going to agree with you."

I laugh, and the last of my tears dry up. That's why I love her. Evelyn Dodge is brassy and bold and says exactly what she thinks. She's a breath of fresh air in this town, and is one of the first friends I made when I moved here.

She's been in the business forever, and was actually Damien's agent back when he was on the tennis circuit. She's held every job in the industry, retired for about five minutes, and is now back doing the agenting thing. She actually represents Jamie. And, unless I'm misremembering, she represents Lyle Tarpin, too.

"I do, indeed," she acknowledges when I ask her. "I'm going to be his date for the evening, actually."

"Really?" Evelyn's usual date is her live-in younger boyfriend, Blaine, but lately he's been spending a lot of time on tour with his paintings. But what I don't understand is why Lyle is going with his agent and not an up-and-coming actress. I've had my fill of gossip for the day, though, so I don't bother asking. "Then I guess you don't want to share my limo," I say instead. "But is it okay if I stay here until it's time to go?"

"I'd love the company. And I've got a girl coming in half an hour to do my hair and makeup. I'm sure we can squeeze you in, too. There's only so much damage control I can do at this point."

I snort. I'm guessing Evelyn's in her late fifties, but she looks absolutely amazing, and I tell her as much.

"And there's another reason I like you, Texas." She glances down at my luggage. "You just leave that there and follow me. We'll get juice for you and something more nutritious for me, and we'll sit on the balcony and exchange sob stories until it's time for hair and makeup. How are you feeling, anyway?"

"Physically? I feel okay right now. The nausea comes and goes." I'd told her I was pregnant by phone the other day when I called to invite her to Sunday brunch, but this is the first time I've seen her in person. "Emotionally, I'm a little under the weather."

"We'll get you fixed up," she says, and I follow her into the kitchen, feeling a bit like a grateful puppy.

Less than five minutes later, we're on her balcony looking out over the Pacific. I'm sipping sparkling cider and eating shortbread cookies, and she's drinking scotch and drawing on an unlit cigarette. "I could find the lighter, but what with you being pregnant, I'm going to at least pretend like I have manners."

"Thanks," I say, forcing myself not to laugh. "I'm glad I came by. Thank you so much for not tossing me out on my ass."

"Oh, please. Misery loves company."

I frown, remembering her earlier "sob story" comment. "Are you and Blaine okay?"

She takes a long swallow of scotch, then refills the glass, forgoing ice this time. "Well, things aren't dead. Let's just say they're on life support."

"I'm really sorry to hear that." I'd met Evelyn in this house when she hosted a show for Blaine, who's a talented artist whose work has a decidedly erotic edge. In fact, Blaine was the artist Damien hired to paint the nude portrait of me. So it's fair to say that I feel something of a personal connection to both Blaine and Evelyn.

"He's a good man, my Blaine. A talented man. But we've been living in two different worlds for a while now. Not age—well, maybe it's partly age. He's barely thirty, and I've crossed the half a century mark. He wants to get out in the world and build his reputation. I've done my homesteading. Now, I want to sit back in my castle and play in the world I've built. I'm not slowing down—well, maybe a little—but I am playing closer to home."

"I'm sorry," I say.

She shakes her head. "No, no, there's no malice here. Just sadness. But there usually is with change. So," she continues, stubbing out her unlit cigarette on the tabletop, "lots of changes on your end, eh, Texas?"

"Damien and I are fine," I say automatically and forcefully.

She laughs. "You're not, or you wouldn't be with me before a premiere party. But you can be not fine without the world crashing down."

I scowl. "It feels like the world's crashing down," I admit as the tears start to flow again.

"Aw, hell, Texas, it's okay. Get the waterworks over with now before we get you fixed all up like a movie star again."

"I'm okay. Just hormones," I say. Then, "No. It's not hormones. It's Sofia."

"Well." Evelyn's eyes go wide, and she sits back in her chair. "Well," she repeats, and I know two things. First, she didn't know. And second, this is damned unexpected. Because it takes a lot to shock Evelyn Dodge.

"So you didn't know she was back."

"Back?" she repeats. "Wait a minute, Texas. You need to start from the beginning."

Evelyn already knows about Damien's past and what happened between him and Sofia. She was there during the bad years when Damien was playing tennis, and his abusive coach was forcing him and Sofia to do those vile things together—often with a camera around. And Evelyn was there for the aftermath, when Sofia had come back with the photographs, threatening to release them if I didn't walk away from Damien.

From the reports, Sofia doesn't even remember a lot of that, because she was in such a dissociative state. But as far as I'm concerned, none of that makes it easier. And when I tell Evelyn that Damien went and saw her without telling me—and then flat-out lied to me—she nods her head and says, "Yes, yes, I see."

"Did you know she was back?" I ask.

"I knew she was doing well," Evelyn says. "I didn't know she was in the States."

"He should have told me. Especially since I've been getting harassing messages." I pass her my phone to show her the email that came in today, and then recite the other three texts for her. "And, gee," I say rhetorically, "who's harassed me in the past?"

"I'm sure Damien's had the same thoughts. He probably hopes it wasn't her. For that matter, he may believe it wasn't her. From what Charles has told me, Sofia's doing remarkably well. Not clinging to the past. Not clinging to Damien."

"I don't believe that," I say, the words coming automatically.

"Which Damien would also know," Evelyn says sagely. "And he might not believe it either. Might be why he waited to tell you any of it. Might be why he went to see her first. Because he wanted to get the lay of the land."

I swallow. She may be right, but I don't want to admit it. "I don't know." I turn to look out at the ocean and the waves crashing up on the shore. A little girl of about three is splashing in the surf as her mother chases her, smiling and laughing. I sigh, then put my hand gently on my belly. "I don't know," I repeat. "Maybe."

She reaches across the table to take my free hand. "Would you like to join Lyle and me in our limo?"

I shake my head and manage a smile. "No way am I spoiling your date."

"Oh, please. That boy's my second choice—and no, I'm not saying Blaine was my first," she adds, obviously reading my expression.

"All right. I'll bite. Who was your first?"

"Let's just say he couldn't join me. Out of the country traveling." Her lips curve into a small smile. "Right about now, I think he's in Ireland."

My eyes widen, and I'm just about to ask when Evelyn lifts her hand to cut me off. I'm not sure if she's silencing me on purpose, or if her mind's just moved on, but it's just as well. I'd rather just savor the idea of Evelyn and my dad getting together.

I'm still smiling at the thought, but it fades when Evelyn asks, "Do you want to call Damien? Tell him you're here?"

"No." I've heard everything Evelyn said, and I know that it all makes sense. But that's a head thing. My heart's still hurting.

"Besides," I add, "this is Damien we're talking about." I think about my new phone. "If he wants to come to me, I'm sure he knows exactly where I am."

"Well," she says with a laugh, "you're probably right about that."

We chat for a bit longer until the girl for hair and makeup arrives. I let her repair my makeup, and then I change into my outfit once Evelyn's in the hotseat. I'm about to put on my shoes when I realize I don't have the anklet, and I remember that I'd been distracted by Damien entering the closet.

I close my eyes and curse softly because I hate the thought of not feeling it against my skin.

Finally, Evelyn's housekeeper comes to her dressing room to announce that my limo's arrived, and I twirl for Evelyn, getting her rousing endorsement before promising to see her at the event, and then rushing toward her front door where the chauffeur is waiting. I stop short when I see him. "Edward? I assumed you'd be driving Damien."

He looks a bit sheepish. "I saw this call come through dispatch, Mrs. Stark."

"Oh. Well, thank you." Edward is my favorite of the drivers that work the Stark International fleet, but he usually works as Damien's personal driver. Normally, I'd advise against leaving Damien to another driver without prior approval, but I'm sure Edward knows as well as I do that since it's me who's the alternate, Damien's not going to say a word.

The thought makes me feel a little smug, as if I've won points in some sort of marital competition.

That feeling lasts only until I step into the limo—and all my points are totally revoked. Because there on the seat, holding out his hand for me, is Damien.

I freeze, not sure if I'm angry or relieved to see him. "Dammit, Damien. I wanted—I just—"

He moves to me, crouching in the limo as he leads me to the seat beside him. "You're hurting," he says gently. "When have I ever stepped away when you're hurting?"

I flash a wan smile. "But you're the one who hurt me."

His shoulders sag, but he doesn't take his eyes off me. "I know. Oh, baby, I know."

"You should have told me."

"I was going to. That day I saw the text flash across your tablet. But once I saw it—once you told me about the others—I knew I had to—" He closes his eyes as if in defense against a horrible thought.

"You thought it might be her," I say. "You went to Santa Barbara to see her. To find out if she'd sent them."

"To make certain she hadn't," he clarifies.

"And?" I ask, but I already know the answer. If Damien thought for a second that she'd sent those horrible messages, he'd have her shipped back to the UK before she had time to draw a second breath. "So why's she here? In California, I mean?"

"You," he says, taking my hands, as if to stop me from running away.

"Me?"

"She wants to see you. Actually, she wants to apologize to you."

"I don't—"

"It's a twelve-step kind of thing."

I nod slowly, absorbing this. "Did you know that's what she wanted before you went?"

He nods. "In general. Charles told me she wanted to see me. He's been working with the court and the institution, arranging her travel and keeping me posted." I remember when she was committed. Damien had asked Charles to continue to represent her. Damien continued to pay the bills, but he needed that buffer.

"Charles saw her first," he continues. "Told me he agreed with the doctors that she was better and that following a twelve-step type program would help cement all the work she's done. It made sense to me, and I want to help her heal, so I went to see her in person."

"You should have told me."

He leans back but keeps my hand firmly in his. "Should I have? I don't know. I thought about it, and, honestly, if it hadn't been for the baby, I would have told you right away."

"Would you have? Because I'm not so sure."

He sighs, then drags his fingers though his hair. "Hell, Nikki, hindsight's twenty-twenty. But I can tell you with absolute honesty that I was trying to protect you. Not from Sofia—I don't believe she wants to hurt you—but from what I knew would make you an emotional wreck. So I decided I should talk to her first. That's when she told me she wanted to talk to you, too."

"You should have," I say with absolute certainty. "You should have told me that she was in California. That you were going to see her."

"It's complicated, baby. She's family. You know that makes it complicated."

"Bullshit." I pull my hand out of his and slide away. "She isn't family. And it isn't fucking complicated."

"Family is what you make of it—you know that."

"Yeah, I do. And she treated us both like shit." I press my hand down hard on the scar on my thigh, well hidden under a layer of silk and sequins. "She tried to taunt me into cutting."

"Do you think I don't know that? Do you think that doesn't haunt me? But I survived my childhood mostly because of her. She's not as strong as you, baby, and she was sick. You've read the original court documents. The doctors' reports."

"And now you say she's better." A heavy fear clings to me. I want her to be better—she's important to Damien. But I'm so afraid that he's wrong. She's smart and sneaky and I don't want to be hurt again. More than that, I don't want Damien hurt again. "How the hell can you be sure?"

"I am," he says. "So are her doctors."

I tilt my head up and blink because I can't cry again. Not after having fixed my makeup twice now. "You love her."

I see the pain in his eyes as he nods. "You know I do. She's like a sister."

I nod slowly, organizing my thoughts. "You walked away from her because of me. Not financially—you took care of her. But emotionally. You just cut her off."

"Of course," he says. "After what she did, of course."

"And now you want to bring her back in."

"Time's passed, and things have changed. She's changed."

"But what if she hasn't? Damien, we're going to have a baby."

He looks as though I've slapped him. "She would never hurt—"

"You don't know that." My voice has risen in pitch.

He draws in a breath, looking shattered. "I would never risk you or the baby. *Never.* And if you tell me to send her away, I will. But she's not asking to be in our life, or our child's. All she wants is to see you. To apologize and move on."

There's an earnestness in his voice that I rarely hear. A vulnerability that I'm certain only I have seen.

"I know I fucked up," he continues. "I know I hurt you. And it's a lot to ask for you to trust me, but—"

I lunge for him, pressing my lips to his for a kiss. Because I need that connection. And, yes, because I need him to stop talking.

His fingers twine in my hair as he deepens the kiss. It's wild. Rough. Teeth clashing, tongues warring, and when I pull back, I'm breathing hard.

"Nikki," he begins, but I press my finger to his lips and shake my head.

"I do trust you," I whisper. "But you hurt me."

"I know. Baby, I know. And I'm sorry. I'm so goddamned sorry."

I nod furiously, blinking again because those damn tears are determined to make one more curtain call. "I trust you," I repeat, forcing the words out past the thickness in my throat. "But I'm scared."

"You don't need to be." He strokes my hair, his eyes never leaving mine. "There's nothing to be scared of."

I don't argue, but I'm not so sure. And I don't know if I'm being stubborn or he's being blind. Maybe it's a little of both. But this is Damien, and in the end, I really do trust him.

"All right," I say, then take his hand in mine. "If you want me to, I'll see her."

He says nothing, just slowly inclines his head. But that's enough. I know that he understands how much seeing her will cost me. And he understands, too, that I'm agreeing only because of him. Because I love him.

I guess in the end, that's reason enough.

"You look beautiful," he says. "Absolutely elegant. I like the lipstick, too."

It's a deep red that is not my usual color, and now I smile slowly.

"Red lips and your blue eyes. You're like living flame."

"But I don't burn," I say, then laugh. "Well, maybe just a little."

He trails his fingertips over my bare shoulder, then down along the plunging neckline so that he is tracing the curve of my breast, making my pulse kick up, and my entire body tremble with desire. "Damien," I say, and I see the answering smile on his lips.

"Shhh." His hand continues down, sliding over the soft, clinging material and making me bite my lip to hold back a moan. Then he moves lower still, until his fingers find the top of the slit that reveals my thigh. "Interesting."

"Damien," I murmur. I'm desperately wet, and I long for a more intimate touch. For his fingers to ease upward and thrust inside me.

"I love the feel of your skin," he whispers as he strokes my thigh from slit to knee and then back up again, touching only what the dress reveals.

I whimper.

The corner of his mouth crinkles. "We're almost to the theater."

I shift on the seat, spreading my legs, my entire body thrumming. "I don't care."

He meets my eyes, his dual-colored ones looking back at me. I see the heat flare in his amber one, but it's the passion reflected in the depths of the pure black one that has my core clenching in response.

Slowly, he moves closer, inching toward me on the seat and then leaning over so that he can cup the back of my head with one hand and brush soft kisses on my neck while his other hand eases higher beneath the dress.

The slit is completely unreasonable, so there's not far to go, and I close my eyes, lost in the sensation of his mouth on my neck, my ear. And his fingers so delicately tracing the soft skin between my thigh and my pubis, coming close to where I want him, but never quite reaching, so that instead of quelling the wild desire inside me, he's fueling it.

"Tell me what you want," he orders, pulling back from my neck.

"I want you to touch me."

"No," he says, a sharp command in his voice. "Tell me what you want."

I gasp as his finger traces along the top of my panties, crossing over my pubic bone and teasing me relentlessly. I feel the shift in the limo as we exit the freeway, and I bite my lower lip. We're close. I should tell him I want him to stop. That there's no time, and we can finish this later.

Instead, I say, "I want your fingers inside me. I want you to make me come."

"I like that answer," he says, his finger slipping over the tiny triangle of my thong to find the string that is really no coverage at all.

I suck in air as he tugs it aside, then strokes my slick skin as I writhe against his touch, spreading my legs even wider.

"That's it, baby," he murmurs as his thumb finds my clit and a wild electrical shock makes me gasp, a precursor of things to come. Then he slips his fingers inside me—two, three, I can't tell—but the sensation of being filled is overwhelming. I crave more—I crave his cock, the pressure of his body over mine as he thrusts deep inside me—but there's definitely no time for that, and I just grind shamelessly against his hand as his thumb continues to tease my clit.

"I see the line," he says, referring to the line of limos that is part and parcel of these kinds of events. "Come for me," he demands. "That's it, baby," he says as he increases the pressure on my clit, the surprise sending thousands of electrical charges to gather between my legs, building and building and then finally exploding with all the power of a star going supernova.

I shake, gasping and clinging to Damien's shoulders as I try to claw my way back to reality. His mouth closes over mine, and I'm vaguely aware that he's readjusting my thong and smoothing my dress.

"I love you," he says as he pulls away.

I smile. "I know."

With a wicked grin, he gently traces my thigh again, this time in the opposite direction. He stops at my bare ankle, swollen today from my pregnancy. "Something's missing," he says.

I start to tell him that I accidentally left it at home when he reaches into his suit coat and pulls the slim box from the interior pocket. He opens it, and the anklet sparkles in the dim interior lighting.

I smile, unreasonably relieved to have it here. "Put it on me?"

He bends to do just that, but he can't get the clasp to connect. With my ankle so swollen, the bracelet is about half a centimeter too small.

"It doesn't fit," I say, stupidly stating the obvious.

"It's okay," he says, tucking it back into its box, and then into his pocket. "I'll keep it safe."

I nod, but it's only for form, and I turn away, ostensibly to look at the crowd lining Hollywood Boulevard in front of the Chinese Theater.

In reality, though, I'm fighting a new wave of tears. Because even though I know it's silly, I can't help but think that not being able to wear the anklet is a very bad omen.

18

We're helped out of the limo by two young men in the kind of black pants and red vests that give the illusion that we're back in old Hollywood and these are eager young movie ushers.

Immediately, the questions begin. Shouts about my pregnancy, about fainting in Dallas, about the children's foundation and the movie and everything under the sun.

Cameras flash wildly, but instead of making me cringe, I simply smile and wave one hand while I hold onto Damien with the other. And as we move down the red carpet, I lean over and whisper, "I'm glad you shared my limo."

"Did I?" he counters. "Funny. I thought you shared mine." And then he pulls me close and kisses me as the crowd applauds.

When we pull away, I'm laughing, and the heavy little knot that had appeared in my stomach when Damien had slipped the anklet back into his pocket starts to dissolve.

The red carpet is set in a serpentine pattern so that it heads from the street toward the pagoda of the original Chinese theater for the photo op and on-camera meet-and-greets, then curves around toward the ballroom where the pre-party is being held.

We follow it, pausing when we see Wyatt, who's set up in front of the step-and-repeat publicity poster with the Stark Children's Foundation logo. There's no time for chatting, but I give Wyatt a quick hug after our photo, then promise we'll see him inside. Then we continue down the path, and everything is so bright and shiny and festive that I feel a bit like Dorothy heading through Munchkinland.

I see Jamie up ahead, and though she's fighting a grin, I can tell she's in heaven.

"And here we have Damien and Nikki Stark, looking ravishing as always," she says, in full-on reporter fashion. She stands by me as she speaks to the camera. "Tonight's event is sponsored by the Stark Children's Foundation. Mr. Stark, could you tell us a bit about what this exceptional organization does?"

"Of course," Damien says smoothly, then gives a succinct rundown of the foundation and its mission to help abused and at-risk kids.

Jamie wraps that up, manages to shift seamlessly from the mission of the foundation to the designer of my dress, and then thanks us both for our time. "And be sure to stay tuned in," she adds before she lets us escape. "There's big news in the Stark family, and you'll get all the scoop in my exclusive interview later this evening."

She flashes a quick grin and I manage an out-of-camera wink as we continue toward the ballroom, and Jamie turns to Academy Award winner Francesca Muratti, who's coming up the red carpet behind us.

"This really is an amazing event," I tell Damien.

"It is."

"Modest much?"

He laughs. "I don't have to be modest. It's not my personal doing. That's why I hire exceptional people."

I just grin. I know how hands-on Damien is about all aspects of Stark International. But the SCF is his passion project, and he's been intimately involved in this event from the get-go.

Lyle Tarpin waves to us from the door, where he's greeting folks individually as they enter the ballroom for the pre-party. Most are celebrities themselves, but some are civilians who bought or were given the pricey event tickets, and in the few moments it takes for us to reach him, I see two young girls practically swoon as they take in his Midwestern good looks and piercing blue eyes.

"I'm never washing this hand again," the taller girl says to her friend as they enter the annex, giggling.

I'm fighting a smile as we reach him. "Look at you," I say. "Reduced to a doorman."

"It was Lyle's idea," Damien says, and I can tell from his tone that he's impressed. Honestly, I am, too. Most celebrity sponsors just mingle inside this kind of party. They believe in the cause, sure. But they don't usually work the door.

"I want people to see how invested I am," Lyle says. "You've done good here, Damien. I'm proud to help."

"We're proud to have you," Damien says as Evelyn steps up to join us, a drink in each of her hands.

She hands one to Lyle, who sets it on a small table beside him, keeping his hands free for greeting arrivals.

"It's the subservient side of my role as his agent," she quips. "He's going to be huge after tonight's premiere. I don't want him getting any ideas about trading me in for a new model."

"Never," Lyle says, shaking hands with an A-list actor whose name I can't remember.

Damien and I continue inside the ballroom, which is set up with standing bars and appetizer stations, all with different themes. The placement of the food and drink stations gently leads party-goers farther inside toward the jazz band and the silent auction.

The main room is decorated with posters taken at the

foundation's summer and after-school camps, as well as images of the kids when they were first brought into the system, usually after being removed from their homes and put into foster care. The laughing, smiling children in the camp photos stand in stark contrast to the somber, sad-eyed faces from the earlier images, and I squeeze Damien's hand in silent recognition of what he'd hoped to build—and what he's truly accomplished.

"Mr. Stark!" An enthusiastic young woman bounces across the room and gives him a rib-breaking hug, then bounces some more. "I got accepted! I'm actually going to MIT!"

"That's wonderful, Karen. I had no doubts at all."

As he speaks, I notice a picture of the girl on the opposing wall. In the photo, she's younger than she is now but older than the other kids pictured—probably fourteen or fifteen. For the most part, she looks the same—certainly, there's no overt sign of abuse—but her eyes in the photo seem dead. Not at all like the vibrant girl now quivering with energy and promise.

She gives Damien another hug and then bounces off. "I wrote her a letter of recommendation," Damien explains.

I look at him innocently. "Your staff does everything?"

He smirks, then shuts me up with a kiss.

"Don't you two look cozy?"

I look over Damien's shoulder to see Sylvia grinning at us, Jackson at her side, with Cass and Siobhan a few steps behind, Siobhan's red hair practically crackling under the lights.

"We are," Damien assures her, then pulls me closer.

"You did good," Jackson tells his half-brother. "This is a hell of an event."

When I'd first met Damien, neither one of us knew that Jackson existed, though looking at the two of them now, the resemblance is remarkable. Not so much in specific features, but in the way they hold themselves. All power and control and defiant self-assurance.

Jackson had been secreted away by their shared father, a man whom I revile. Jackson had known about Damien, but had been ordered by their father to stay quiet.

Jeremiah Stark had not only kept Damien away from his brother but he'd also known about the horrible abuse that Damien had suffered as a child at the hand of his coach. He'd allowed it to continue because Damien's athletic success fueled Jeremiah's financial dreams. And now that Damien has made more of himself than anyone ever anticipated, Jeremiah is still constantly in our lives, popping up here and there as he looks for some new angle that will squeeze a dime out of his son. We haven't heard from him in months, though, and I have to assume that the rumor that he's gone to visit friends in Australia is true.

"We're going to see what kind of trouble we can get into bidding in the silent auction. I'm hoping a cruise is up for grabs," Sylvia muses. "I've never been on a cruise."

"*She's* looking to get into trouble," Cass corrects from behind them. "I'm looking to see how many bidders I have so far."

Cass is Syl's best friend. She owns a tattoo parlor and donated a package to the cause. And, according to Syl, is about the most frugal person on the planet.

"Don't worry, sweetie," her girlfriend Siobhan says with a wicked gleam. "I'll bid if no one else does."

Cass laughs. "Thanks. I was hoping to not be the silent auction wallflower, though."

I can hardly imagine Cass being a wallflower anywhere. She's tall and dark and exotic. Today, her long hair is dyed black with a single streak of blue that matches the tail feathers of the magnificent bird tattooed on her shoulder.

"Well, I'm bidding," Syl says.

"Another tat?" Cass asks her.

Syl shakes her head mischievously. "I'm thinking it'll be a

gift for someone," she says with a meaningful glance at Jackson as she taps the base of her neck.

"We'll see," he says in a tone that sounds more like, "No way in hell."

I laugh. "Thank you both for donating," I say to Cass and Jackson, because Jackson donated a residential design, which considering his standing in the architectural community, is pretty damn generous.

The girls head on to the auction set-up, but Damien pulls Jackson aside, mentioning something about building a rec center on some property in Ventura County that the foundation is looking to acquire.

I linger behind, and am glad I do when Dallas, Jane, and Noah step up to say hi. I'm congratulating Jane again on the movie—and on her incredible red dress—when Damien returns. He kisses Jane's cheek and shakes hands with Dallas and Noah.

"I appreciate the ticket," Noah says. Noah Carter is the tech genius that Damien has been heavily recruiting to join Stark Applied Technology.

"Anything to bring you over to the dark side," Damien says.

Dallas shakes his head in what is clearly mock regret. "I thought he was my friend, but he's leaving me for the lure of a more tech-centric job."

"What exactly did you do for Dallas?" I ask Noah. Dallas Sykes is the CEO of a longstanding department store chain, and before he married Jane, he'd earned the nickname the King of Fuck because of his reputation as a playboy heir who romanced women, spent money, and basically wasted his life.

That's not the Dallas I've gotten to know, and I'm curious about what exactly is hidden under that fine-looking exterior.

"There's tech in retail," Noah says noncommittally.

"And he'll still do freelance work when I need him," Dallas adds, with a clear edge to his voice.

"Always," Noah says. "You know how invested I am."

Dallas nods, and I try not to show how completely baffled I am.

"I know I shouldn't talk work," Damien says to Noah, "but can I borrow you for one second?"

"And I've lost him already," Dallas says with a laugh as Noah steps aside with my husband.

"He didn't bring a date?" I ask Jane. "I'm certain we sent him two tickets."

"He gave the second one to the receptionist at his hotel. Apparently, she's a huge Lyle Tarpin fan."

"That was sweet. But why not—"

"His wife was just pronounced dead," Dallas says softly. "About three months ago."

"Oh. I had no idea."

"She, well, she went missing seven years ago in Mexico. He's been holding out hope, but it's been rough."

"I imagine," I say, my heart aching for him. I can't even fathom surviving if I lost Damien.

"It's one of the reasons he's been talking with your husband," Dallas says. "I'll be sorry to lose him, but I'm glad he's coming down here." As he speaks, he puts his arm around Jane's waist and pulls her close. "He's . . . well, he's broken right now. And he's a good friend. If this move is what it takes to help him heal, then I'm all for it."

Noah and Damien come back, and this time when I look at Noah, I can glimpse the sadness in his eyes. He's an exceptionally good-looking man, with rich, auburn hair and the kind of athletic build that demands attention. So it's easy to overlook the loss that clings to him. But it's there, and it breaks my heart a little.

The men drift away as Jane and I continue to chat, talking about her movie and the party and all the incredible dresses we're seeing here tonight.

"Are you hot?" I ask, picking up a program and fanning myself. "I'm dying. Want to walk over to the bar for a drink?"

She peers at me, then down at my ankles. "Assuming you mean water when you say drink, I'm all for it. Mostly, I think we should find you a chair. You do look a little pale."

We move to the bar area and snag one of the cocktail tables. Jane heads off to get wine for her and water for me, and while she's gone, Steve and Anderson plunk down in two of the chairs opposite me. "You guys," I say, giddily. "I haven't seen you in ages. I'd hug you, but there is no way in hell I'm standing up again right now."

"I hear congratulations are in order," Steve says. He's a working screenwriter who never had a movie produced until they hired him to do some rewrites on *The Price of Ransom*. Now, he and Jane share credit for the screen adaptation of her book.

"They are. Just a few months and I'll be a parent, too. How's Lily?"

"Amazing," Anderson says, pulling out his wallet and opening it to show off the picture of the smiling little girl with dark curls they adopted almost two years ago.

"We're thinking she needs a sister," Steve says.

"We weren't," Anderson clarifies. "But my sister and brother-in-law just got back from China with their son, Matthew. He's precious. I'd bore you with a picture, but my phone ran out of charge. Anyway, Matthew is the reason Lily may not stay an only child."

"Lily was privately adopted," Steve says. "But we'd adopt from China in a heartbeat if they'd let us. It's a ridiculous system."

Anderson pats his hand. "Give it up, sweetie. There are a lot of kids who need homes." He returns his attention to me. "We can't adopt from China," he explains. He leans forward as if to convey a secret. "We share the love that dare not speak its name."

Steve rolls his eyes. "In other words, China doesn't like that Lily has two daddies."

"I'm so sorry," I say. "But Anderson's right. There are a lot of other kids who need you."

Steve waves it away. "Didn't mean to get morose or political on you. Especially when you're on the nest. When are you due?"

"I'm not exactly sure. My first official appointment is Monday. But the doctor in Texas thinks I'm about ten weeks along."

"And are you hoping for a boy or a girl?"

"Either. But I think it's a girl."

"Well, I have to give a personal thumbs up to little girls," Anderson says. "But don't be disappointed if you're wrong."

I laugh. "A miniature Damien Stark? How could I be?"

"A mini-me?" Damien asks, coming up to join us. "Hi, Steve. Anderson. Do you mind if I steal our girl? Jamie wants to do the interview before Lyle and I talk to the crowd."

"Sure," I say. "Keep me posted," I add to the guys. I'm about to relay our conversation to Damien as we walk away when he tugs me into the shadows. I'm expecting a quick kiss before we go see Jamie. Instead, he says, "I talked with Bruce."

"My old boss? Giselle's ex-husband?"

"One and the same."

I frown. "How does he feel about Giselle being here?" I haven't actually seen her tonight, but since she donated the Glencarrie, I'm sure she's around. "And did you tell him about the texts and the email? What does he think of her state of mind lately? Could she be sending them? Even though she's got money now? She's bound to still be pissed at you and me." My words come spilling out, but it won't make me sad to learn that Giselle's the one harassing me. I'll just be glad to have answers.

"I did tell him," Damien says. "Considering he went through a lot of the earlier shit with you, I didn't think you'd mind." Damien's right. When I'd worked for Bruce, the paparazzi had basically stormed his office to get at me, all because his asshole employee, Tanner Gates, wanted to make a little easy money by leaking my location—and in the process, punish me for doing my job better than him. Then later, Bruce learned that his estranged wife Giselle had done essentially the same thing, selling Damien and me out to the press in order to make a buck.

So, no. I don't mind Bruce knowing about the harassment. "Well?" I press.

"He doesn't think it's Giselle. He confirmed my thoughts, actually. She's happily married now with the bank account to prove it, so any lingering jealousy of your windfall from marrying me has disappeared."

I see the amusement dancing in his eyes. "What are you laughing at? It really was a hell of a windfall." I ease closer and kiss him lightly, my palm against his chest. "Only I'm not talking about your money."

He kisses the tip of my nose. "Bruce did have one interesting theory, though."

I lean back, intrigued by the serious tone of his voice. "What? About the messages, you mean?"

"Apparently, Tanner was in the running for the Greystone-Branch project. Or at least the company he now works for submitted a proposal."

I stumble under the force of that revelation. Every message has sounded like a disgruntled competitor.

"I intend to have a little talk with the bastard," he says, and I grab his arm, shaking my head.

"Don't do anything rash," I say. "It's not like he's the only one it could be. Please," I add when he gives me a look that very clearly suggests he is not convinced. "Promise me you won't fly off the handle."

His nod is curt but firm, and I'm just about to pull him into another hug, when Jamie rushes up to us.

"Hello? What, did you get lost? Come on. We're going to do this outside so we can have the theater in the background. And so we can get a few shots of the crowd. Are you okay?" she adds, peering at me. "Your makeup's about to slough off."

"I'm warm," I say. "Blame the hormones."

"My producer has some powder. We'll get you camera ready."

Damien casts a worried eye my way, but says nothing as we hurry outside. Someone shouts for Damien, then for me. The voices rise to a chorus of indistinct sounds, and my head fills with a high-pitched whine as the producer comes over to dab powder on my face.

Then one voice stands out. A familiar one calling out, "Nichole Louise!"

Mother?

I whip around, my blood going cold, but with the camera flashes, I can't see faces.

I turn back, then reach out to grab Damien's wrist. "Did you hear?" I ask.

"What?"

"I—" I pause, the world starting to shift beneath my feet. "Sorry. Light-headed."

"We should find you some food. Here, hold onto me."

"We can wait a few minutes," Jamie says. "It's okay. We'll just—*Nikki.*"

I look up at her, my stomach cramping violently.

"Oh, God, Nikki. Your dress."

I look down—and see that my white dress is stained with blood.

"Roll camera!" the producer yells.

"Don't you fucking dare," Jamie retorts. And as she shoves the lens away, Damien scoops me up and sprints for the theater door, all the while yelling for the usher to call an ambulance.

And throughout it all, the only thing I seem to be able to do is cry.

19

A miscarriage.

Dr. Tyler's words echo through my head, and no matter how hard I try, I can't seem to drown them out: *"I'm so sorry, Mrs. Stark. You've had a miscarriage."*

A miscarriage.

They've given me something, and my head feels fuzzy, my body heavy. My arm is cold where the IV liquid is dripping in, and the hand that Damien clings to is numb.

"Is it true?" I whisper to him. "We've really lost the baby?"

He closes his eyes, his expression like cracked glass. "It's true," he says as tears trail down my face. "Sweetheart, I'm so, so sorry." He starts to reach for me, but there is a rail on the bed and tubes and rolling contraptions. After a moment, he sits in the chair again, his sigh joining the hum and rattle of the machinery.

"Why don't I remember getting into bed? I remember the ambulance, but nothing after we got to the hospital."

The last thing I recall with any clarity is Jamie pointing out the blood on my dress and Damien calling for an ambulance. I know I didn't pass out—I can remember the paramedics, the shrill of the siren, Damien's voice as he called the emergency number for the obstetrician I was supposed to see this coming Monday. But everything I remember is filtered through a drugged, gray haze. And though I recall arriving in the ER, nothing after they started the IV is clear.

"Damien?" I press. "What did they do to me?"

He rubs the fingers of his free hand against his temple, and when he speaks, the words come slowly, and I know that he's fighting for control. "Dr. Tyler got here right after we did. He took care of you, sweetheart, but he had to—he had to make sure you were okay, and they put you under for the procedure."

"Oh." I swallow. "There's something else wrong, isn't there?"

"Sweetheart, no." He stands, then lets go of me long enough to fiddle with the rail of the bed again, trying to lower it. It refuses to cooperate, and he curses and sits farther down, beside my legs, his hand resting on my thigh.

"Miscarriages happen all the time, Damien, especially in the first trimester." I have no personal knowledge of this, but I've read enough that I'm pretty confident. "They don't admit you for a miscarriage."

"They do when you donate as much to this hospital as I do." His hand tightens on my thigh. "There's nothing else wrong." But he says it in his boardroom voice, as if he expects to will it and make it so.

And while Damien is certainly powerful, even I don't think his control reaches that far.

The door opens, and Dr. Tyler steps in. He's the obstetrician that Dr. Cray in Texas contacted for us. I hadn't met him before today, and my memory of him from earlier is choppy. But he has kind hands and a warm manner, and his smile is full of comfort.

"What else is wrong with me?" I demand while he palpates my abdomen.

"Nikki—" I hear the censure in Damien's voice, but I know I'm right, and my fear is confirmed when Dr. Tyler nods slowly.

"I'm sorry," he says. He turns to Damien. "I'm afraid your wife is correct. You have a bicornuate uterus," he says, looking at me. "It's a type of Müllerian defect," he continues, although at this point all I'm hearing is that I'm broken. When I hear him say, ". . . of course, the prognosis isn't entirely negative," I tune back in.

"I'm sorry, what?"

"I know this is a lot to take in," he says gently. "But even though most women with this condition miscarry with a statistically high frequency, it's still possible to carry a child to term. And if you do make it past the first trimester, the risk of miscarriage decreases significantly."

"You're saying if I get pregnant again, the odds are that I'll lose the baby before the third month. Over and over and over again."

My voice cracks as I speak, and I see sharp lines of pain cut across Damien's face.

"That doesn't sound like a good prognosis at all," I whisper.

He inclines his head, acknowledging my words. "I know, Mrs. Stark. I'm truly very sorry. You can—"

But I don't want to hear anymore. So I just roll over, shut my eyes, and let the pull of my own pain drag me back down into sleep.

I sleep in the hospital until Saturday morning, then doze in Damien's arms at home with our cat, Sunshine, curled up beside me, her low purr filling my mind so that I don't have to dream.

Throughout the day I drift, getting out of bed only to go to the bathroom. I stand at the sink, staring at my eyes that seem sunken. My skin like paper. Damien's razor sits in a cup on the counter, and I think how easy it would be to just twist the handle and open the compartment that the blade fits in. To take the blade out and run the honed edge gently over my skin. Just a shallow cut. Just enough to make a few beads of blood rise.

Just enough so that I know that I'm alive.

But I don't.

Because right now even that seems like too much effort, and I move like a sleepwalker through the darkened room and back to bed.

We rarely close the blackout drapes, preferring to keep the door open to the balcony that looks out over the ocean. But today they are closed, rendering the room so dark I can barely see my hand.

Today?

Maybe it's tonight. I don't know. All I know is that I want to get sucked under again. I want Damien's arms around me, and I want to drift away, falling far into a place where the pain and the loss can't reach me.

And so I slide back into bed and mold my body to his. His arm drapes across my waist, and I hear him murmur my name. I don't answer, and as soon as I close my eyes, sleep grabs me once again.

I don't know how long I sleep, but I wake to the vague sound of movement in the house. A moment later there is a light tap at the door and beside me, Damien stirs, then lifts his head. "Come in."

The door opens slowly, sending a triangle of light cutting across the room. Gregory, Damien's longtime valet and overall house manager, steps inside. "I'm very sorry to disturb," he says, his voice low, "but Mrs. Stark's mother is here."

I sit up, pulling the sheet up to my neck like a shield as Damien holds me tightly. "No," I say. "I—I'm sorry. Can you tell her I'm not available?"

He nods solemnly. "Of course."

He leaves, and the room returns to black.

"We don't have to see her," Damien says, stroking my shoulder. "But we should get up, sweetheart."

"I know. But I can't." I close my eyes against the darkness in the room, and slide down into the darkness inside me. "Not yet."

He says nothing, but a moment later I feel his lips brush my temple as his arm slides over my waist to pull me closer. And I lose myself in the safety of his embrace and hide from reality for just a little bit longer.

20

A day passes. Then another and another.

I sleep, and I sleep, and I sleep some more. And each time I wake, Damien is there. Holding me. Watching over me.

I slide in and out of dreams, finding comfort in his presence. In the cool sheet against my hot skin. In the darkness that permeates the room, revealing nothing of the outside world, and hiding even time herself under a fake, permanent night.

But then my safe cocoon disappears, and I open my eyes to find a room bathed in light. A brisk ocean breeze is blowing in through the open patio door, Sunshine is bathing herself at the foot of the bed, and Damien is nowhere to be seen.

I have no idea what time it is—or what day it is, for that matter. My eyes ache from the unfamiliar light, and my head throbs in protest of a returning consciousness that is not entirely welcome.

Still, as much as I'd like to stay hidden, I know that it's time to ease back into reality. To sit up. To put my feet on the floor. And then, finally, to walk out of this room.

I can do this, I think, and then I push myself upright. I sit on the edge of the bed and press my hand to my belly, then choke back a little sob because there is no child growing there any-more. And that's so sad and horrible, but what makes it worse is the knowledge that there probably never will be. That I'll never have Damien's children. That the life I'd started to see spreading out before me has been shut down so brutally.

But it's time to leave this bed. I don't have to shed the sad-ness, but I need to start moving through the world.

I stand, feeling creaky after spending so many hours asleep, then head into the bathroom wearing the loose sweatpants and tank top in which Damien must have dressed me. I splash water on my face and generally try to come alive, and when I emerge, I notice my phone sitting on the table near the bed-room door.

I pause in the doorway as I scroll through my text mes-sages—condolences from pretty much everyone I've met in my life, either in a text or sent by voice mail. I know I should reply, and I will. Soon.

Just not quite yet.

My stomach growls and I try to remember when I last ate. I have a vague memory of Damien bringing me soup, but I don't know how long ago that was.

I put my phone back on the table, then head out of the bed-room and toward the kitchen, thinking that if I have an appetite that must be a sign that I'm healing.

I expect to see Damien in the third-floor sitting area, but it's empty. Well, not empty. In fact, every flat surface is covered with flowers and plants and unopened boxes. I blink, staving off tears as the reason for these gifts stabs me straight in the heart. But I look at the cards as I pass. A pot of daisies from Jamie and Ryan. A beautiful climbing vine from Sylvia and Jackson. A spray of wildflowers from Evelyn. And a small bon-sai garden on the pass-through bar that opens between the sitting area and the third-floor kitchen.

There is an unopened card with it, and I slide my finger

under the flap, then pull out the thick cardstock. It's from Damien's father, Jeremiah, and there are only two words—*I'm sorry*. But whether he means about the miscarriage or all the trouble he's caused for Damien and our marriage, I don't know. Still, I appreciate the sentiment.

I head into the kitchen, and as I walk that direction, I hear Damien's voice drifting up from the mezzanine below. He's on the phone as if it were just another day. But, of course, it *is* another day, and I'm the one who is stuck. Who wants to just pull the blinds and go back to sleep and run away from it all.

Coffee, I think. And with a pang I remember that I can actually drink it now. Gallons and gallons if I want.

There's a pot already brewed, and I pour myself a cup, then take a long, bitter swallow.

I put the cup down and open the drawer beneath the coffee-maker. It's filled with kitchen knives, the ones with mismatched handles that aren't pretty enough for the knife block that rests on the small island. I stand there, just looking down at those blades, and though I know I shouldn't think it—though I definitely shouldn't want it—I know that they will help.

"You're up." Damien's voice is soft behind me, and I shove the drawer shut and turn to face him, certain that he can see my guilt. He comes to me, his eyes searching my face. But he doesn't ask. Instead, he pulls me close, and I cling to him, and we stand that way in silence for what seems like forever.

"What day is it?" I finally ask.

"Wednesday," he says. "Late afternoon."

It takes me a moment to process his words. That means it's been over four days since the miscarriage. Four days during which I'd completely checked out of the world.

"It's okay," he says, his lips brushing the top of my head. "You needed the time."

"You were working," I say, and though I don't mean it to, my words sound like an accusation.

He nods. "Today, yes. And some yesterday. There were things I had to take care of." He takes my hand. "Now I'm going to take care of you."

He leads me to the table, then tells me to sit. I comply, and then I watch as he moves about the kitchen. He doesn't ask what I want, and I'm glad, because right now I don't think I have the capacity to make a choice. And when he slides a plate with buttered toast and a simple cheese omelet in front of me a few minutes later, I think it is the most perfect meal in the world.

He sits with me in silence as I eat. "Better?" he asks when I've cleaned the plate, and I'm a little surprised to realize that, yes, I do feel better. Stronger, at least, and that's a step in the right direction.

"Good," he says when I tell him as much. He stands and holds out his hand for me. "Walk with me."

We walk in silence on the beach, on and on for what seems like forever, coming back to the house only as the sun is about to set and the ocean starts to turn orange and gold.

"It's beautiful," Damien says as we sit on the pool deck on an oversized lounger and watch the world shift into night.

The words form a hard ball in my gut. "It feels like nothing should be beautiful anymore," I whisper.

"No," he kisses my forehead. "I like it. It means there's hope."

I blink, and fat tears spill down my cheeks. "Is there? Because it doesn't feel like it."

"Sweetheart." He pulls me close, his voice as lost as I feel.

"I feel like I'm broken," I admit. "The baby's gone. And so is any real chance of me ever having another one."

"No, sweetheart. No."

But I just shake my head, not willing to hear him. "I should be relieved," I say harshly, my eyes on the pool deck. "I'm not cut out to be a mother."

"Bullshit. That's your mother talking."

"No. It's me." I look at his face, lost in the gray of dusk. "Do you know how many times I thought about cutting today? All those knives in the kitchen? Your razor in the bathroom? The utility knives in the garage? The pocketknife you keep in the top drawer of your dresser? It's as if they've been calling my name.

"That's not someone who should be a parent," I continue.

"*No.* Dammit, Nikki—"

"I want to cut, Damien. I want to cut the pain right out of me. I don't because I know I shouldn't and I know you're here. But I want to. I want to so damn much."

He pulls me roughly to him, and I cling to him as I cry. Tears burn down my cheeks, and it feels like a million knives are slicing me up on the inside.

As the sobs rack my body, he holds me close, rocking me gently. And through it all, I wonder if I'm ever going to stop hurting again.

I don't know how long we sit like that, but I must have drifted off because the next thing I know, he's carrying me into the bedroom and tucking me into bed.

"Sleep," he murmurs, and as he bends to kiss me, I hear my phone ping with an incoming text message. I automatically reach for it, not really caring, but he shakes his head. "Don't worry about it. I'll get it. You sleep."

And though I don't know how I can possibly sleep anymore, I do—at least until I'm wrenched awake by someone shaking my shoulder violently.

"Nikki!" It's Jamie's voice, and I squint up at her. "I'm so sorry, but Nikki, you have to wake up. We have to go."

"What?" My voice is hoarse, confused.

"We have to go," she repeats. "Damien's been arrested."

21

I'm in the closet frantically pulling on jeans and a T-shirt when Jamie rushes in. "It's okay," she says. "Charles just called. They're on their way back here."

I sag to the carpet. "Thank goodness. What happened?"

She shakes her head. "I don't know. Charles called here for you, but no one answered the phone. So he called me. Actually, he called Jackson first, but Stella said they were out so I guess that put me on deck. And he said I had to bring you to Beverly Hills because Damien had been arrested." She shrugs. "And now I guess he's not. Or Charles posted bail or something."

She reaches a hand down to help me up, and I grab hold, letting her pull me back to standing. Then I throw my arms around her and hug her tight. "Thank you," I whisper. "I'm sorry I haven't called you back. I haven't called anybody back."

She peels me off of her. "Don't be stupid," she says, with typical Jamie bluntness. "We love you. All we want is for you to be okay." She makes a face. "That, and for Damien not to end up in a maximum security prison."

I wince, but I'm smiling. And I realize that despite the odd circumstances, it's my first real smile since the miscarriage.

I follow her out of the closet and head into the main part of the house. "He was here with me last night. How could he end up arrested?"

Even as I speak, I notice a difference in the way I feel. Less numb. More focused. And for one brief, ridiculous moment, I wonder if Damien ran out into the world last night simply so that I would be forced to crawl out of my funk.

"Do you want me to poke around online? See if there's any gossip?"

I shake my head. "No. Maybe. I don't know." The idea of seeing some horrible story splashed across social media just depresses me. And most of the time, the reporting's inaccurate anyway. "What about asking the police directly? Your station has reporters on the police beat, right? Can they make a call for you?"

She presses her lips so tightly together they disappear.

"Jamie?"

"I kind of don't work there anymore."

I gape at her. "What? Since when?"

But even as I ask the question, I know the answer—since she pushed the camera away from me and denied her network my story.

"Oh, James. I'm so sorry."

"Not your fault," she says firmly. "Assholes. Who trades on shit like that?"

"But—well, what are you doing now?"

"I'm a woman of leisure," she says. "Fortunately, your husband pays my husband very well." She holds her hands up in front of her face as she examines her nails. "I'm thinking about pursuing a career as a lady who lunches."

Her voice is light, but I know her too well.

"You'll find another gig," I say gently. Of course, what I mean is *thank you*.

"Yeah, well, nobody fucks with my friends."

I'm about to swallow her in a body-slamming hug when I hear the beep of the front door's keypad. I trade a glance with Jamie, and we both race that direction.

Moments later, I'm on the stairs, watching as Damien comes in, followed by Ryan, Charles, and Evelyn. I fly the rest of the way down and into Damien's arms. "What the hell happened? Where were you?"

"Tanner Gates," Evelyn says, moving farther into the sitting area. "The little prick."

I whip around to face Damien. "What the hell? You promised you wouldn't fly off the handle."

But Damien just pulls my phone out of the back pocket of his jeans, then passes it to me.

I have a vague memory of a text coming in last night, and I cringe with trepidation as I open the app.

Are you humble now that you've lost it all?

I try to draw in a breath, then realize I've covered my mouth and nose with my free hand. "So it really was Tanner," I say. Then I frown, confused. "But if he was sending the messages, why was Damien arrested?"

Damien's mouth curves into a wry grin. "That might have something to do with the fact that I broke his nose."

Jamie takes the phone gently from my hand, reads the message, then curses. "Okay, you guys," she says as she goes to Ryan's side. "What exactly happened?"

"I read the text last night," Damien begins. "I was sure it was Tanner sending those damn texts. He has access to your mobile number. The messages started when you interviewed with Greystone-Branch, then escalated when you got the contract, and he didn't. He knows damn well the job is time sensitive, and with—" His voice cracks. "And with what's happened, I'm sure he's certain you'll pull out."

I shake my head. "But the email with the pictures of you and Sofia. How would he have even gotten that?"

"Social media," Jamie says. "Honestly, I'm surprised you didn't see some there before they hit your inbox."

I make a face. "Because I spend so much time on social media?"

"That's why I thought he sent it to you," Damien continues. "To make sure you saw it. To twist the knife just a bit more." He rubs his temples. "As far as I was concerned, every goddamn piece fit."

"Go on."

"I went to his apartment," Damien says simply. "And we had a little chat."

"You punched him in the face?"

"Actually, I slammed him against the doorframe," Damien says. "But the result was the same. And then the bastard called the cops."

"Jesus, Damien, you—" But I don't know what to say. That he can't fly off the handle like that? That I can't survive if he's tossed in jail because some judge wants to make an example of him?

Except . . .

"Wait," I say, still confused. "You were arrested for punching him, but surely they'd be lenient because he was harassing me. Right?"

"Where was the proof?" Charles asks. "Damien went over there on an assumption. And I was all set to bail Damien out when Tanner stepped up and refused to file a complaint." He glances toward Ryan. "Thank him if you want to know why."

"Why?" Jamie and I demand at exactly the same time.

"Fortunately, our boy Tanner isn't too bright. While Damien was with the cops, I told the little shit that I'd traced the messages back to a burner phone he'd purchased by using a combination of satellite triangulation and cross-coordinating that with the phone registration number as shown on his electronic credit transaction log."

Jamie gapes at him. "You can do that?"

"Hell no. But you're not the only one in the family who can act." He grins. "Then I told him that if he didn't back the fuck off, we'd publicly reveal his harassment and use every dime at Damien's disposal to make sure he never gets a better job than flipping burgers at a gas station grill."

Jamie claps. "I love it."

"I got him so worked up, he pulled the phone out from where he was hiding it and turned it over to me. Then he dropped the charges."

"We won't have any more problems from Tanner," Damien says. "And I'm seriously considering giving Ryan a raise."

"Hell, yeah," Jamie says.

"Here's the thing," Ryan adds. "He swears he didn't send the email with Sofia's pictures. And what I've seen on his burner backs that up. He gave me access to his computer and his regular phone, too, and there's no sign of the email or the image."

"Under the circumstances, it's doubtful he'd lie about that," Charles says.

"So that means . . ." I trail off, looking to Damien.

He sighs. "It means we still don't know who sent those pictures to you."

Evelyn waves a dismissive hand. "That one went to your email. Could be anyone at all, for no reason other than that they follow you two in the news and have a mean streak."

"Or some crazed girl who's never met Damien but thinks that he should have married her," Jamie adds.

"Or Giselle," I say, because no matter what Bruce and Damien say, I still don't trust that woman.

"Maybe," Jamie says. "But don't worry about it. It was one email. Let it go, at least for now."

I have to agree that's wise advice, but Damien frowns. "Easier said than done." He slips an arm around me and kisses my cheek. "You guys have coffee or breakfast or whatever you want, I need to go crash."

"Sure," I say, but as I watch him go up the stairs, a cold knot of worry builds inside me. And I'm so lost in my thoughts that I actually jump when Evelyn comes from behind and puts her hand on my shoulder. "It'll all be okay, Texas," she says when I spin around. "In the end, everything will be just fine."

I'm still clinging to those words ten minutes later after I've seen everyone out. Thankfully, they all turned down coffee, probably realizing that all I wanted to do was crawl back into bed beside Damien. But when I go to the bedroom, there's no sign of him there. I hug myself, certain that he's gone to the second floor and the kids' rooms—a place I haven't been since the miscarriage.

I steel myself and go down the back stairs that open behind the kitchen only to find that he's not down here, either.

For a moment I'm baffled—and then I realize that I know exactly where he's gone. I take the stairs to the first floor and then hurry through the huge commercial-grade kitchen to the massive gym that takes up almost half of the first floor.

Sure enough, Damien is there, and he's beating the shit out of a punching bag. He's taken off his shirt, so he's now barefoot in only his jeans. The muscles in his back tighten with each thrust, and he's completely oblivious to everything but the assault on that leather bag.

He's not wearing gloves, and he didn't wrap his hands, and even as fast as he's punching, I can see how red and raw his knuckles are. I make a small sound the next time his fist makes contact with the bag, and he turns to me. His eyes are wild, and I'm not even sure he realizes I'm there. Then he drops to his knees on the mat, my name a soft whisper on his lips.

I hurry to kneel in front of him. "I'm sorry," I say. "I'm so sorry."

His brows quirk down. "For what?"

"I've been so selfish." A tear snakes down my cheek. "I've been so lost in my own pain that I didn't think about yours. I'm sorry," I repeat, knowing that he wouldn't have flown off the rails so dramatically if he hadn't been just as wrecked as I am. "I'm so, so sorry."

For a moment, he just looks at me, and I see both under-standing and heat in his eyes. We need this, I think. We need each other. We're both raw. Both broken. Both in desperate need of release.

I feel my body tense in expectation. He's going to pull me to him. Take me. He's going to use me to make himself feel better, to grab control by controlling me. He needs it, and God knows I need it, too.

But that wild touch doesn't come.

Instead, he simply pulls me close and holds me.

And there in the circle of his strong arms where I've always before found comfort, I feel as hollow as I did in the hospital.

22

After staying up all night, exhaustion finally claimed Damien, and he's been crashed in our bed for hours. Now it's lunchtime, and I'm pacing the house like a caged tiger, unable to settle. And certainly unable to sleep even a minute more.

I feel off. Hell, everything feels off, and I don't know what to do to turn it right again.

I hardly ever use our gym, but I'm at such a loss that I'm actually considering going down and hitting that ridiculous bag, when my phone rings. I snatch it up, grateful for the distraction, and see that the caller is Frank.

"I'm so sorry," he says the moment I answer. "How are you doing?"

"I'm getting better. It's been hard, but it's getting better. Either that or I'm getting used to the pain."

For a moment, I just hear him breathing. Then he says, very softly, "I should have called sooner, but I—I feel like I should have some wisdom for you. Some fatherly advice. But I don't. I don't know what to say at all except that I'm sorry."

"That's good, though. It helps." It doesn't, of course, but

that's what people do. One says they're sorry. The other says it helps. And they both feel like they've played their part.

I frown, disgusted with myself. Even in grief, I'm wearing a mask. Mourning Nikki. And I don't want to be that girl around this man. Now that he's in my life, I want it to be real.

"What would you do?" I ask, surprising myself with the question.

"What?"

"In a tragedy. What would you do? To feel better. To get through it."

"Oh."

I can tell I've put him on the spot, and I regret it immediately. I'm on the verge of telling him never mind when he answers, speaking very softly and thoughtfully.

"Something just for me, I think. Maybe it won't make me feel good right away, but it lets me believe that whatever it is will pass."

"Like what?"

He exhales. "Aw, honey, I don't know. I'm sorry. I've got no business offering you half-baked advice."

"No," I say quickly. "No, I appreciate it. And it helps." Weirdly, it does. I like that he didn't spout some pre-packaged platitude. That part of his answer is telling me that I have to find my own way. "Really," I say.

"That's half the reason I didn't call earlier," he admits. "I wanted to give you time, sure. But I also didn't know what to say."

"No," I say. "It's good. Really."

"Should I come back? Would that help?"

I'm touched by the tenderness in his voice, and I smile. It feels good. Unfamiliar, but good.

"No," I say. "You don't need to do that. Just knowing that you would helps, though. And I'll see you when get back."

"All right, then. That's a plan. You call me if you need anything at all."

"I will."

"Okay, then," he says gruffly. "And Nikki?"

"Yeah?"

He hesitates. "I—I'm glad I called."

My smile broadens. "Me too."

I hang up the phone, and I do feel better. Not perfect, not healed, but better.

There's still a hollowness inside me, though. A space I need to fill. I think about what he said about finding something I love, and after a few moments of frustration, I finally know what I need to do. I grab the Leica camera Damien gave me when we first started dating, and head down to the beach.

I walk for a while and take random shots—the water, some seashells, some teens playing volleyball, two college-aged guys way out on the water on surfboards.

But none of it's what I want to see through my lens.

I may only be an amateur photographer, but I know what I like and what I have a talent for, and I've always been drawn to faces. As if the camera can help me see what's beneath the mask that people inevitably put on.

But it's not that revelation I crave today. I want to capture young faces. Chubby cheeks and wide eyes. Faces full of hope. Faces that are looking toward a future.

I walk back in the surf and then up the path that leads to our house. I don't bother going inside; I just head straight to the garage and get into Coop. My plan is to go to the Palisades and have my fill of quality time with my niece and nephew.

Except that's not where I end up.

I'm not sure why, but when I reach the turn, I just keep driving, going on and on until I find myself in Pasadena at the gate for the fifteen acres of mostly undeveloped land owned by the Stark Children's Foundation. Right now, it's overflowing with foster kids from all over the country who've come here for one of the many week-long summer camp sessions.

I greet the guard, who lets me in without question, then head to the main building that houses the offices, cafeteria, and classrooms. I stop in long enough to let the staff know that I'm going to be taking a few photographs on the property, and then I start to walk the grounds.

All of the children have releases signed by their guardians on file that allow us to use the photos in promotional materials, so this isn't the first time that I've photographed the kids at camp or during other foundation functions. Granted, it's not usually my job, but I'm here often enough that no one will think it's odd.

Today, I'm not interested in taking publicity photos. Instead, I'm searching for hope where there was fear. Joy where there used to be loss.

I crave finding that in my viewfinder, then capturing it, as if I can bottle that kind of vibrant hope against outstanding odds.

My favorite place to sit and watch is a set of bleachers near the soccer field. Today, the kids are running relays, and I use my zoom lens to zero in on the children waiting their turn. I focus on one boy who, obviously bored, is trying to touch his nose with the tip of his tongue. Then I pan the group slowly, soaking in the expressions and the faces until I see one that is all too familiar.

I freeze, my heart pounding as I slowly lower the camera.

She's wearing a blue staff shirt and a white SCF ball cap. But even without the zoom lens, I know that face.

Sofia.

For a moment, I just sit there, certain that somehow I've been transported to some horrible alternate universe.

Then I slip my camera strap over my arm, stand up, and hurry down the bleachers.

I'm halfway to my car when she calls my name. "Nikki! Nikki, please wait!"

I tell myself to just keep going, but it doesn't matter. My feet stop, and I turn to find myself looking into her familiar pixie face and untamed auburn curls.

"You," I say stupidly. "I thought you were in Santa Barbara. Honestly, that was plenty close."

"I'm sorry," she says, and the words sound genuine. "I came here after Damien and I talked. I told him this was part of, well, of my recovery. Helping out here for a week of camp and—well, then I heard about what happened to you and, um, I guess I wasn't sure if I should stay or go."

She looks down at the dusty ground. "I came to apologize to you. I want to apologize to you. And I couldn't call and ask Damien what to do. Not with everything being so . . . you know. So I stayed."

Her words have been rolling off her tongue, and when she comes to a sudden stop, the silence is almost brutal.

"You hurt me," I say, my voice dripping with incredulity. "You tried to make me cut. And you tried to break Damien and me up—hell, you almost succeeded."

I see her throat move as she swallows.

"And as if that weren't enough, you pretended to be my friend. And now you want me to stand here and let you apologize so you can feel better about yourself? So that you can get back in Damien's good graces?"

Her head moves in the tiniest shake. "I—I didn't . . . I mean, you're right. You're so right."

But I'm not even remotely appeased. I jam my hand into my back pocket, pull out my cell, and thrust my phone at her. "Is this you? Did you email those pictures of you and Damien? Because I can damn sure see you trying to twist me up that way."

"What?" I'm watching her face as she answers. The crease in

her brow. The tilt of her head. Either she really is confused, or she's one hell of an actress.

Of course, I already know that she's a hell of an actress.

"This," I say, opening the email so she can see both the message and the photos. Her eyes widen, then she thrusts the phone back at me as if it were a snake.

"No! Nikki, no, I swear. I wouldn't do that—not anymore."

"Maybe Damien believes you, but I don't."

As I watch, tears fill her eyes. "I don't blame you," she says. "But I swear on Damien's life that I didn't send those pictures. And I'll go back to England—I will. I just— it's just that I've worked so hard. So many doctors. So many treatments. I was so fucked up—I mean really, seriously fucked up. But I clawed my way back—and all of that work was so that I'd really and truly mean it when I told you that I'm sorry. Because I am sorry, Nikki. I like you—I really do. And I screwed it all up."

I say nothing, but I do clench my fists. Not because I want to lash out at her, but in defense against the way her plea is breaking through my armor.

"I'm glad Damien has you," she says. "You make him happy, and that's all I want. Really."

I just look at her. We both know that's not all she wants.

She shakes her head as if I'd actually spoken aloud. "Before . . . I was off. And maybe I won't ever be completely right. In my head, I mean. But I'm fighting and I'm winning and I'm not going to give up on me."

She draws a deep breath and shakes out her arms a bit, like she's been wound up tight until now and can finally relax. "So, anyway, that's just my way of saying I'm sorry. And, well, that's it. It's not enough, I know, but I hope you'll accept my apology. But if you won't, I get it."

Her words wash over me, sincere and dangerous.

"I—"

I swallow, unsure of what I want to say. I, what? That I

understand her fight? That I enter that same battlefield every time a blade tempts me?

That I've spent a lifetime trying to prove myself professionally? To prove that I'm worthwhile even though my mother always suggested that it was only my looks which were of any value at all?

That I started out damaged, too, but that I've fought it every day?

Should I tell her that I think we're more alike than I realized—or that I'm comfortable with?

And that, right or wrong, I believe her apology is sincere. And I believe that she didn't send that email.

In the end, I don't say any of that at all. I just say, "Apology accepted."

Somehow, I think she understands.

Sofia and I walk beside each other back up the path that leads to the administration building. We're not together, not really, but we're moving in the same direction, keeping more or less in time with each other.

We reach the heavy wooden door that leads into the main reception area, and she pulls it open for me. I step through with a quiet murmur of thanks, then stop in my tracks just over the threshold.

Damien is right there, standing at the main check-in counter. Warm relief flashes on his face when he sees me—and then immediately transposes into shocked wariness when Sofia enters behind me.

"Damien," she says, her voice bright with surprise. As I turn to look at her, she takes a step toward him, then stops and bites her lower lip. She looks at me, then draws a deep breath. "I meant it," she says. "Everything I said. I hope you know that."

A flicker of a smile touches my lips. "I'm glad I ran into you."

She nods, then looks at Damien again. I expect her to go to

him, but she stays where she is. "I'm so sorry about the baby, D. But I gotta go. I—I need to get back to the kids."

She gives me one final glance, then scurries out the way we came in.

Damien and I stay right where we are. The receptionist behind the counter looks at him, then at me, then mutters "excuse me," and leaves as well.

Now it's just me and Damien in this small, stone room.

"D?" I say, both because I'm curious about the nickname and because the air is too damn thick.

"An old nickname. Her father only used last names. But with my dad traveling the circuit with us, it was confusing. So I became D and he became J."

I take a step toward him. "So you're not starting a boy band?"

He moves a single step toward me. "No."

"Too bad." I move closer.

"Do you want me to serenade you?" Another step and he's right in front of me.

"No."

He slides his fingers into my hair and pulls me closer. "Do you want me to kiss you?"

"Yes," I say—or I try to. His mouth captures mine before I finish the word, and I fall into the kiss, into his touch. Into the passion that we have always shared and that has always saved me. And that even now, when we are both damaged and raw, can keep me steady.

I'm breathing hard when we reluctantly separate, and I press my cheek to his chest as he strokes my hair with one hand, his other arm holding me close against him.

"I didn't know she was here," he says. "I'm sorry."

I tilt my head up. "You didn't?"

"I told her she could work the camp—part of the twelve-step thing I told you about. But once everything happened . . . well, I didn't realize that she'd actually made the arrangements.

I wouldn't have—anyway, I'm sorry if you were caught off-guard."

"So you didn't come here looking for her?" It's not until I've actually voiced the words that I realize that was my assumption. After all, I hadn't left a note telling him where I was going, and he hadn't texted asking where I was. So presumably he'd come here for some other reason. Probably to tell her that he'd finally told me about how she wanted to apologize to me face-to-face, but that with the miscarriage, now probably wasn't a good time.

But Damien's shaking his head, dispelling my assumptions. "I came for you. You know I'll always come for you."

"But how—" I cut the question off. Of course he knew where I was. Somehow, he always knows.

He pulls his phone out and shows me the screen with his primary contact list. He taps an icon next to my name and a map pops up. And right there, on the grid-style map, is a tiny picture of me in the middle of what is the Stark Children's Foundation.

"Clever," I say. My phone does the same, of course. I just never think to use it.

"And my apology still holds," he continues. "I'm sorry if Sofia blind-sided you."

"No. No, it's okay. She . . ." I trail off, searching for the words. "She seems better. And she seems sincere."

I watch his face and see a flicker of hope. It's been hard for him, I know. He loves her—not like he loves me, but she's important to him the way Jamie and Ollie are to me. And I'd love them both even if they went off the rails.

"She won't ever be my best friend," I tell Damien, because I'm pretty damn certain about that. "But I think we can move on from here."

I watch as relief flares in his eyes, then sigh as he pulls me close for a long, deep kiss. I melt against him, and when I feel his erection press against my belly, every cell within me fires. I want him—we've held each other tenderly every night since the miscarriage, but it's been far too long since we've made love.

Now, I crave him, and a wild desperation washes over me, setting my senses on fire and making me wish that we were someplace other than the reception area of a children's foundation.

We're both breathing hard when we break the kiss, and our eyes lock on each other's for what feels like an eternity. My heart thuds in my chest, and I can feel the blood pounding through my body.

I want to get out of here

I want to drop naked onto the floor and not care who sees.

"With me," Damien says brusquely, tugging me with him as he hurries past the desk and into the foundation's main hall. We reach the end of the corridor, then enter his private office. It's rarely occupied—he tends to work from here only when he's holding a foundation-related meeting or courting donations—but it has a desk and a couch.

Best of all, the door locks.

He closes it, then flips the latch, then presses me against the wall, his hand cupping the back of my neck. "Nikki," he murmurs, before his mouth closes hard over mine.

His other hand slides down my body, cupping my breast, tracing my waist. His fingers move as he hitches up my skirt, then slides his hand up my thigh as I gasp against his mouth, then cry out when he cups my sex.

I whimper, craving a more intimate touch, and he doesn't disappoint. His fingers slide under my soaked panties, and he thrusts them inside me, then finger fucks me in time with his tongue teasing my mouth.

My fingers dig into his shoulders as I moan with need. I want more—so much more. Wilder, more intense. And when he picks me up and carries me to the couch, I anticipate a savage build, a violent claiming.

I know how much the drama with Sofia has weighed on him. Then there's the miscarriage, the arrest, my mother—with all of that, he must be about to burst. But instead of coming to me, he's been boxing in the gym, pounding out his frustrations.

I know that he's been trying to let me heal. But physically, I'm fine now, and I need that intensity. That desperate, primal wildness that has always been our strength.

I need it, and because I know he does, too, I expect him to take me brutally. To use me as an antidote against all his fears and frustration.

And yet he doesn't.

Instead he pulls my panties off and settles me on the couch. He kisses me, strokes me, teases. Every touch is a treasure. Every stroke ignites my senses, making me crazy with need. And with every touch, I expect him to ratchet it higher.

I'm so damn wet, my thighs slick with need. And when I spread my legs, he thrusts inside me, kissing me as he makes love to me, fingering me to take me closer to the edge, pushing me higher and higher until an unexpected orgasm rocks through me, and I shatter into a million pieces, then sigh beneath him, warm and sated, as he murmurs that he loves me.

He's made love to me beautifully, with a gentle sweetness that fills me with a tender love and a glowing happiness—and a hint of dissatisfaction.

I curl against him, frustrated with myself, because I know that I should feel nothing but joy that we are healing. But I can't quite get there. Because underneath the happiness, I can't deny the tiny niggle of fear that he's ignoring what he needs because he sees me as something fragile and breakable.

Most of all, I can't escape the fear that we'll never truly get past this tragedy if we can't take from each other exactly what we need.

23

I spend the next three days using the third-floor kitchen as an office. The table is my desk, and while my laptop is the center-piece, all of my documentation for the Greystone-Branch project is spread over the polished wood.

I sit for so long, my ass goes numb, and I drink what must be several times my weight in coffee. I sleep only when I have to, and my food is all delivery.

Damien has said he'll cook for me—which is tempting as he has surprising skill in that area—but I've told him that if I'm getting back to work, then he must, too. And I'm not going to accept food charity if it keeps him away from his empire.

I'm not entirely sure that he's getting much work done, but he does spend a few hours at his desk on the mezzanine level every day, and longer than that juggling conference calls.

By the fourth day, though, he stands behind me with his hands on my shoulders. "You need to slow down," he says. "You're going to make yourself sick."

I think of what Sofia said. About how she worked hard and clawed her way back. If she could salvage her sanity, then I can damn well save my business. "I've lost too much already," I tell Damien. "I'm not losing this contract, too."

He pulls up the chair beside me and sits down, then presses his hand over mine so that I'm forced to stop typing. I look up, irritated. Because, frankly, I really am screwed here, and if I don't hit my next marker, I'm going to have to pull out of the project. Wait any longer, and it would be unprofessional; I'd be leaving Greystone-Branch in a terrible mess because there'd be no way for me to finish on time.

"You can't push yourself like this for the next three months."

"I made a commitment. More than that, I worked my ass off to get this job in the first place. I'm not letting it slip away." I know I'm bordering on unreasonable, but I can't stand the thought of losing the job after the baby. It's too much—just too damn much.

He nods a little sadly, then presses a kiss to my forehead. "I know. But you're pushing the limit."

"Dammit, I don't have a choice." I lean back and hold up my hands. "Sorry. I don't mean to snap, but I'm under the gun, and I need to concentrate. I'm working on a tricky section and the coding is complicated."

He sits for a minute studying my face, then he nods. "All right. What can I do to help?"

I cock my head. "In case you've forgotten, you have a universe to run."

"Nikki—"

"If you really want to help, let me do this. I just need time. Please, Damien. That's all I really need."

For a moment, I think he's going to argue some more, then he stands up and walks away with my coffee cup. He returns a few moments later with a coffee refill and a frozen Milky Way.

I force myself not to laugh. "Thank you, Mr. Stark."

"Any time, Ms. Fairchild."

He heads for the elevator that is the quickest route to the

mezzanine, and I turn back to my coding. A few moments later, I hear the murmur of his voice as he starts to make phone calls. I tune him out and dive back in because there is more code to be written than there are hours in the day.

I'm deep in the thick of it when I hear the doorbell, which is odd because guests can't actually get to the door without going through the security gate. But I assume that I was so deep in concentration that I didn't hear the intercom, and that Damien took care of it.

I'm just about to dive back into work when I hear male voices downstairs and then two sets of footsteps coming up. I glance down at my ratty yoga pants and ancient Sea World T-shirt and mentally groan. Damien may think I'm stunning all the time, but as a general rule, I like to at least brush my hair.

I've just decided to make a break for our bedroom to quickly primp, when they step into view. I freeze in the middle of the kitchen, confused. Because Damien is standing with Noah Carter.

"Hi," I say, looking between the two men and wondering why Damien didn't tell me we were having company. "Did you guys have a meeting planned?"

"You said you needed more time," Damien says. He gestures to Noah. "I brought you the next best thing."

I stare at him, then at Noah. Then back to Damien. "All right, I'll bite. What are you talking about?"

"I have a month before my contract starts with Stark Applied Technology," Noah says as if that explains everything.

It doesn't.

I look to Damien, then hold out my hands in an expression that says *I got nothing.*

"Hire him," Damien says. "I promise you won't regret it. You have coding to blow through? The man's a genius."

"Hire him," I repeat as I let Damien's suggestion sink in.

Then I smile, first at Noah, then at my husband. "You really are amazing."

Damien grins. "So they say."

"All right," I say to Noah. "You're hired."

"Excellent." He cocks his head. "You do have major medical and a decent severance package, right?"

I roll my eyes and point to the kitchen table. "Your workstation. Come on, I'll show you what I'm doing, and we can set up a file-sharing protocol."

He nods and follows me. Damien lingers, leaning against the refrigerator. "Don't look so smug," I say. And then I mouth, *thank you.*

He actually does look a little smug when he leaves, but I realize I'm smiling, and since that feels pretty good, I decide to give it a pass.

Noah's as sharp as advertised, and having him around gives me a little time to breathe. Over the next few days we hit the deliverables, outline the next phase, and I even have some time to poke around on the Internet, exploring a few ideas that have been bubbling in the back of my mind.

And for the first time in a long time, I genuinely feel good.

I pause for a moment, just to let the pleasant emotion linger. It's been far too rare lately, and although it's wonderful to feel my heart lighten, there's a little bit of guilt there, too. Like I shouldn't be ready to laugh again yet.

I push the guilt aside, though. I don't need it. Not yet. Not when the sorrow still comes in waves.

The intercom buzzes, and I leave my seat across from Noah to go and check in with the guard. "Hey, Jimmy. Do we have a delivery?"

"A guest, Mrs. Stark. She says she's your mother?"

He says it as a question—one I don't particularly want to answer.

"Oh. Well, okay. You can send her down."

Damien's in the gym, but I call him over the intercom, and by the time I transfer a couple of files to Noah and head downstairs, he's waiting for me in the entryway in gray sweats and a UCLA T-shirt.

"I can send her away," he says. "You don't even have to see her."

I shake my head. She'd been on my mind before, but since the miscarriage, I've been thinking more and more about family and parenting and mothers and daughters. "No," I say. "No matter what else she is, she's my mother. She's family."

"She hurt you."

I nod because there's no denying that truth. "I know. But Sofia hurt *you*. She hurt both of us." I lift my head to look at Damien. "She's family, too, right? Isn't that what you said?"

I can see on his face that he wants to argue—and honestly, I know the arguments he'll make because I can make them, too. That Elizabeth Fairchild was never a real mother to me. That I was a pretty dress-up doll to her, never a little girl. And that, once I became inconvenient, she had no use for me. At least not until I married Damien. Only then did I become interesting—and even then, only until she realized she wouldn't be getting any of Damien's money.

I know all that—I do. And yet there's still a hole in my heart that is the shape of a mother's love. And though I know that my sister fell through that hole and never managed to crawl out again, I can't escape its dogged temptation.

"Sweetheart," he says, but in a voice that makes it clear he knows I've already decided. "You're going to get hurt."

"Maybe," I admit. "But you'll be here if I do."

When the doorbell rings, I jump, then hurry to let her in, pausing only for one deep breath before I open the door wide.

"Mother." I hesitate, then step to the side. "Come in."

"Elizabeth," Damien says. "What brings you here all of a sudden?"

She flashes her most charming smile at him. "You look as dashing as ever, even in such unappealing attire. And, of course, I came because of the tragedy."

She turns to me. "I saw you at the premiere," she says, sweeping inside then standing still as she tilts her head from side to side, taking in the whole, huge room. "I was one of the plebeians in the crowd. I called out to you—did you hear?"

"I heard you, Mother. I was a little preoccupied, what with losing my baby and all."

She makes a *tsk-tsk* noise. And though she says nothing else, I get the distinct impression that she's criticizing me for making such a spectacle of myself.

I hold tight to Damien's hand, grateful when he says nothing, but simply squeezes back.

My mother sighs heavily as she crosses to the sofa and takes a seat. "I wanted to come see you at the hospital, but I didn't know how long you'd be there."

"It's fine," I say. "I wasn't in the mood for company."

"You mean you didn't want to see me. No, don't argue," she says, though I've made no move to contradict her. "You probably still don't, but there are times when a girl simply needs her mother."

I press my lips together and nod, and all the ways I've healed over the last few days seem to slip away from me as tears fill my eyes. Because she's right. I wouldn't trade Damien and my friends and all of their support for anything, but I can't deny that I would have liked a mother's arms around me through all of this.

I'm not so foolish, though, to think that the mother in my imagination is Elizabeth Fairchild. But even so, there's a tiny little bud of hope growing inside me, and I don't know whether to nurture it or crush it under my heel before it once again grows thorns.

"You sold your house," Damien says, presumably to fill the silence that is starting to grow. "Have you moved to LA?"

"I have," she says, then offers me a picture-perfect smile again. "I've been here for a while."

"Where are you living?" he presses.

Mother looks annoyed, but she smiles prettily. "I haven't settled yet. Right now, I'm in a small rental in a darling section of the Valley."

He nods as if she's said something fascinating.

I assume he's just trying to be polite. I'm much bolder. "You've been watching me," I accuse.

Her fingers twist in her lap. "Yes, well, you must admit that our last time together didn't end well. I was afraid you wouldn't want to see me. But I very much wanted to see my little girl. I wasn't certain you'd noticed me. I hope I didn't disturb you?"

"No," I lie, fighting a frown, because she might be telling the truth. I sent her back to Texas before our wedding, making it perfectly clear that she had no business meddling in my life. "Not in the least."

Mother clasps her hands in her lap. "Yes, well, despite everything, I had to come. I'm of an age now, you see. And one thinks about such things." She looks at Damien, and her voice trembles as she speaks. "I want very much to repair my relationship with my daughter."

She looks down, and in the brief moment that I can see her eyes, I think I see tears.

My stomach clenches, and I think of Sofia, who I believe, and my mother, who I want to believe, but I can't quite make the leap.

"I don't want to disturb you," she says. "I know how much your work means to both of you, and it's the middle of the day. I just wanted to say that I'm here. And I wanted to give you this." She reaches into her purse and pulls out a small box, then hands it to me.

I open it and find a familiar gold necklace with an engraved charm hanging on it. A heart with the initials NLF.

"You're still my little girl," she says.

"I remember this," I say. "I thought it was lost."

"It's been in my jewelry box for years," she says lightly, as if I should have thought to look there when I was nine and had believed the gift from my sister had gone missing. "You refused to take it off even for school. We couldn't let it get lost, could we?"

I feel a slow burn begin inside me, and I clench my fist tightly, letting my fingernails dig into my skin. I'd been frantic about that necklace, which I'd believed really had been lost. I feel wrong and unbalanced, and I know that without Damien beside me to hold my hand and keep me centered, the first thing I'd do after my mother left, would be to find a blade and cut until this horrible feeling flows out of me.

I stand quickly, scared by the direction of my thoughts. "I—I should get back to work."

My mother's brows rise, the silent equivalent of an order.

"Thank you for the necklace," I say dully.

"Walk me to the door, sweetie," she says, then looks at Damien. "You don't mind, do you?"

It's clear that he does, but I just nod, signaling that it's okay, then fall in step beside my mother.

"You must know that things happen for a reason," she says as we pause in the open doorway. "Babies take so much time, and we both know how selfish you can be about the things you want to do."

I just stare at her.

"Now, Nichole, you know I'm right. You mangled your own body simply because you wanted to inconvenience me."

I stand frozen—stunned by her words. *Inconvenience* her? I was drowning in the pageant life. Forced to be her wind-up toy, her performing monkey. I'd begged to stop, begged to cut down to only one pageant each year. Begged for any kind of relief she'd allow me, but she'd denied me everything.

I'd already started cutting by then—it was the only way to hold onto my sanity. To keep myself anchored to the ground and not flying off into some horrible, melancholy nightmare. But I'd been careful, never using a blade where it might be revealed in an evening gown or a swimsuit. Because I knew what the fallout would be if my mother learned of my weakness.

Finally, though, I'd had enough. And when I knew that I simply couldn't take it any more, I'd taken a blade to flesh that would be exposed. My hips. My thighs. The worst is on my inner thigh—a still-angry scar from when I cut too deep and, frantic, had rendered my own First Aid with superglue, duct tape, and an Ace bandage.

That was the end of my pageant career. And, as far as my mother was concerned, a huge affront to her reputation and social standing.

"But, of course, you're very successful," she continues calmly, as if she's not tossing words out like grenades. "Your business. Your rich husband." She leans in to kiss my cheek, and though I cringe back, I'm stopped by the doorframe. "Just remember what happened to Icarus when he flew too close to the sun. Maybe losing this baby was your way of crashing back down to Earth."

I want to lash out—to tell her she's a fool and wrong and a terrible excuse for a mother.

But I can't find the words. All I can think of is how much I craved the blade over the last few days. How much I wanted the release it would bring. How much I needed it to get me back to center.

And so I just stay quiet. Because if she's telling me I have no business being a mother, then she just may be right.

24

Damien rests his hands on my shoulders as the door closes behind my mother. Slowly he begins to knead my muscles, and I sigh, wishing he could squeeze out every bad feeling she's left inside me.

"Do you want to tell me about it?" he asks.

I close my eyes, from both the ecstasy of his touch and the agony of her parting words. "Yes. No. Later." I draw a breath. "It's just my mother. Just the usual."

He stops massaging. "Are you sure?"

I keep my back to him, because if I turn around, he'll see fresh pain in my eyes, and we've both suffered too much already. "I just want to get back to work," I say truthfully. "I don't want to think about her another minute."

He turns me in his arms, his eyes searching my face. I'm not sure he's convinced, but he knows me well enough to not push. At least, not yet.

Since work really is the best remedy for my mother, I go back upstairs to where Noah is still deep in the thick of it. I check in with him, then dive back into coding, losing myself in the architecture of the project and letting the rest of the world simply fade away.

There's so much to do that it's easy to fall into a rhythm and let work rise to the top, acting as a balm against the lingering pain.

We work steadily for the rest of the week, and by the time Friday rolls around, I'm confident this thing is going to come in on time. For that matter, everything is looking better. Life has slid back into a rhythm. Damien's started going to the office again instead of working from home, I've had four excellent phone interviews with potential new hires, and Noah and I are moving through tasks in the Greystone-Branch project outline with a pace that exceeds my expectations.

We've just competed another milestone, in fact, when Noah rises to stretch. I stand, too. "You know what?" I say. "Let's knock off early."

He leans to the side, his head cocked and his brow furrowed as he looks me up and down. "You look like Nikki Stark . . ."

"Ha, ha." I grab my coffee cup and head over to the coffee-maker to refill it. "We're on track and doing great. So let's take a step back and enjoy it. Take the afternoon off. Then over the weekend Damien and I can move this mess to my office," I say, indicating the spray of papers and stacks of file folders. "We can finish out the month there, and before I send you off to work at Stark Tower, I'll get you to help me prep for my first progress presentation in Dallas. Sound good?"

"Sounds great. And I'm happy to have an afternoon and weekend."

"You should do something fun. Go to the beach. Learn to surf. Or I could find someone to show you around. Who knows where it might lead."

I hope he takes me up on it. The more I get to know him, the more I like Noah. He's sharp and funny and focused. But he's also quiet and haunted.

"Thanks for the offer," he says. "But I promise I know how to fill a weekend."

I bite back a frown, because I really don't believe that. Still, I remember what Jane told me about his missing wife who has only recently being declared dead. Even if Noah had been on the verge of moving on, I can see that change in the status quo stopping him in his tracks.

But I like him well enough that I wish I could help.

"Are you sure you want to wrap for the day?" he asks as he packs up his stuff, pausing to reach down and scratch Sunshine on her head. "I can stay. We can blow through another chunk."

"No," I say firmly. "Break time."

I happen to know that Damien has a light schedule today. And now that the world is starting to look brighter around the edges, I intend to take a different kind of break from work.

"Fair enough." Noah takes off his glasses and tosses them onto the table, making me think of a superhero shedding his mortal persona. And when he flashes a charming smile, it only cements my belief that it's a shame he's not interested in dating. Because I can think of a dozen girls at Stark International who would fall for him in a heartbeat.

He grabs his laptop bag and heads for the stairs, all the while running through a list of things we need to be sure to tackle on Monday.

"Go," I say laughing. "And try to spend at least five minutes this weekend doing something other than thinking about computer code or engineering or whatever new gizmo you're inventing in that mind of yours."

"Yes, boss," he says, and I roll my eyes, biting back a grin.

As soon as he's gone, I sit at the table again, then reach for my phone. Sunshine trots over and leaps up onto my lap, and I rub behind her ears, getting her little motor going, then call Damien.

He answers on the first ring. "What can I do for you, Ms. Fairchild?"

"I sent Noah home," I say, in the tone of an invitation.

"Did you?" I hear the rising heat in his voice and feel my own body tightening with need. "That's very interesting information."

"From what I hear, you're an expert at taking information and turning it to your advantage." I lift Sunshine and deposit her on the floor so that I can stand. I'm anxious to move, my mood brightening simply from this heated flirtation with my husband.

"It's a reputation that's well-earned. I may have to prove it to you."

"How fast can you get here?"

"Time me," he says, and I can't help but laugh.

"The clock is ticking, Mr. Stark."

"Soon, Ms. Fairchild." And then he's gone, and I'm left grinning like a crazy person in my kitchen, because it feels like we're really healing. That we're shifting back to us again.

I hum as I open up a bottle of wine, then pour myself a glass. I've just taken a sip when the doorbell rings, and I frown because that makes no sense. Since Gregory is at the market, I start down the stairs. I'm just about to call the gate to ask how someone got all the way to the door when a text from Jimmy comes in telling me that there was a delivery and he authorized them to leave it on the porch.

Curious, I pick up my pace. I'm actually wondering if Damien arranged a surprise as I open the door—and then I freeze when I see the thick, flat box and the words stamped on the side: *Baby Crib, White, Zoo Animal Design.*

An unexpected punch of grief hits me with the force of an attacker. My body goes limp, my wine glass slips from my hand, and I stumble backward, my hand going over my mouth as tears stream down my face.

No.

The word slams through me so damn hard that I feel bruised inside. And that's all I can think. Just—*no.* There's nothing else. Just gray. Just loss.

Just my feet pounding up the stairs and my body moving through the house, and my knees aching as I fall hard on the floor of my closet, because I want to get away. I want to hide.

Everything was getting better. I'd believed *I* was getting better. But I'm not.

Dear God, I'm not.

One symbol, one memory, and everything's fallen apart. And the world is rushing in around me, proving that all the healing we've done just was camouflage. I'd believed that my return to work was proof that I was getting better. But it was just a mask. A salve for the pain. And now that the bandage has been so brutally ripped away, I'm not sure that I can stand it.

I want Damien—I *need* him. But he's not here, and I'm so goddamn lost.

My chest aches from gasping—from trying to catch a breath through the body-wracking sobs. I need something—no, not *something.* I need pain. Release.

I need to cut.

Just one simple swipe of a blade to release the storm that is raging inside me. Nothing more than steel against skin. Just a quick flick and it would be done. Just one cut. Just one clean line of blood.

It would be enough.

And it would be so easy. So very easy.

I'm breathing calmer now, and I climb to my feet, then go over to the library-style ladder. I move it down the rail to the corner, then climb to the top. There's a decorative hat box in the back corner, and I draw it to me, then carefully climb down and put the box on the floor.

I kneel beside it, then yank off the top. The box is full of memorabilia, and I paw through it, looking for the small leather case of antique scalpels I'd tucked away here. Not because I ever thought I would need it, but as a reminder that I had the strength to never touch it again.

But I don't have the strength. I'm not strong at all.

It's there, the brown leather smooth from handling. I take it out and hold it in my palm, imagining the gleaming blades. The way the sharp instruments will twinkle like fairies in the dim light of this closet. And the way the cool steel will feel against my too-hot flesh. The release. That sharp, exquisite pain that can conquer the raging inside me.

Slowly, I unzip the case and stare at those perfect, beautiful blades.

I can do this.

I need to do this.

I want it to do this. I want it, dammit. I want it, I want it, *I want it*.

Except I don't.

What I want is Damien, and with a scream of frustration so raw it hurts my throat, I hurl the scalpel set across the closet. The still-open case thuds against the wall by the open door, jarring the instruments from their compartments and scattering them across the floor.

I start to lunge for them, then force myself back with a fierce cry of, "*No*."

And then I curl up by the granite island, press my forehead to my knees, and cry.

I'm still on the floor when I feel Damien's hands on my back, then gripping my waist. "Did you cut?" He turns me over and then runs his hands down my legs, his movements crisp, his eyes full of purpose. "Dammit, Nikki, the floor is littered with blades. Did you cut?"

"No." I choke the word out. "I wanted to—I think I meant to—but no. No, I swear, no."

He pulls me violently to him, then presses kisses to my lips, my face, my hair. He cradles me hard against his chest, holding me so tightly I can barely breathe. "Nikki, oh, God, Nikki. I came home. The door was open, and the box for that damn crib was right there. Then I saw the shattered wine glass, the shards everywhere. I couldn't find you, baby. Christ, it took forever to find you."

His voice breaks, and he bends his head so that his forehead is pressed against mine. "I'm so sorry I wasn't here, baby. I'm so, so sorry."

I don't realize that I've started crying again until I try to speak and choke on my own tears. I give up and just cling to him, letting the tears flow as he rocks me.

"I thought I was better," I say when I can finally squeeze out words. "I thought I was healing. I didn't . . . I don't . . ." I shake my head and try again. "I don't know what happened. I saw the box, and I just—" A wet sob breaks out of me, and I shudder, then look down, feeling stupidly ashamed.

"No," he says, tilting my head up. "Tell me."

I meet his eyes and see my own pain reflected there.

"It's more than just losing the baby," I whisper. "It's that I probably can't ever have one."

"Sweetheart," he whispers, the word holding so much pain I fear I'm going to start crying again.

"We lost more than a child, Damien. We lost the possibility of one. It's like I lost us the future. *Our* future."

"No," he says firmly. "Sweetheart, no."

"I thought I was healing," I tell him again. "But I don't know how to move forward. I can't," I say as fresh tears trickle down my cheeks. "I can't do this without you."

"Baby, I'm right here."

"No. *No*," I repeat, and this time my voice comes out strong, fueled by the same sadness and frustration that pushes me to my feet. "You're *not* here," I say. "But dammit, Damien, you need to be. You're just as ripped up as I am, don't you see that?"

I pace the length of the closet, my heart pounding in my chest. "You went after Tanner. You're beating the shit out of that punching bag downstairs. You're hurting and you're finding relief everywhere you can—but not with me, Damien." My voice breaks. "Not with me."

He looks at me, and as he rises to his feet, I see a new kind of pain behind his eyes. A pain of recognition. Of regret. "Nikki—"

But I'm not done. "You're treating me with kid gloves," I say. "But dammit, you know what I need. And you need it, too. But you're denying us both because you're treating me like some fragile fucking thing. But I'm not fragile—I'm strong. You're the one who's always telling me so. But I'm strong *with* you, Damien. Without you I break. Without you, I'm that," I say, pointing to the scalpels on the floor.

"Please," I beg. "Don't hold back. Don't turn away from us. You see me so clearly. You always have. So don't pretend you don't understand. Help me," I beg, my words tumbling out like a waterfall, wild and rough. "Help me be strong, and you—"

But I don't finish, because he's pushing me back, slamming me against the rack of clothes, his hands tight around my upper arms, and his mouth attacking mine with such fervor that our teeth clash and I taste blood.

"Is this what you need?" he asks, breaking away long enough to tug the sash from my silk robe that hangs just a few feet to his right. "For me to take you hard? To fuck you? To use you? Do you want feel the sting of my palm against your ass? Do you want me to tie you down so that there's no escape? So that you have to feel everything? Pleasure, pain, unrelenting and unforgiving?"

"Yes," I whisper, closing my eyes. He knows that's exactly

what I need, and the fact that he's finally back rips through me like a storm. I'm wildly turned on, and desperately relieved. My body is on fire. My breasts feel heavy, my nipples tight. And I'm so damn wet.

He slides his hands down my arms until he reaches my wrists, and then he yanks my arms up. I gasp, my eyes flying open, and I melt a little bit more at the open passion and heat I see on his face. He uses one end of the sash to bind my wrists together, and then ties the opposite end to the dress-height closet pole, so that I'm forced to stand upright, my arms above my head.

I'm wearing casual work clothes—a simple silk tank top paired with a pencil skirt, and he teases his fingertip down from my wrist to the shoulder strap of the tank, then traces the outline of the V-neck against my skin. "Do you like this shirt?" he asks, but before I can answer he's grabbed either side of the V and pulled it apart like a jacket. The fragile material rips open to expose my bra. The sound is sharp and dangerous—and wonderfully enticing.

"I'll buy you another," he says as he tugs down my bra, freeing my breasts, then squeezes one nipple so hard I cry out.

"Tell me why," he demands, still pinching my nipple. He bends forward to whisper in my ear. "Tell me why you thought about cutting. Tell me why you need the pain."

"Because—" I can't get the words out past the sensations that are flooding me. Pain. Pleasure. Heat. Desire.

A hot cord seems to connect my breast to my cunt to my wrists to my lips to every cell in my body. I'm so turned on that even the whisper of a breath over my clit would send me over the edge—but I don't want that. Not yet. I want to stay here, balanced on a knife edge, teetering in that netherland between pain and pleasure, desire and satisfaction.

Damien knows that—dammit, he's always known that. And thank God he's back and finally—*finally*—taking me there.

"Tell me," he presses. "Why do you need the pain?"

"To turn it around," I say, forcing the words out. "To draw it in and turn it around and battle it down. To know that I can win." I meet his eyes. "To control it," I say, "and turn something hard into something exceptional."

"Pain into pleasure," he murmurs, pinching my nipple even tighter. "Is that what I give you? Is that what you want?"

"Yes," I say. "God, yes."

"Good girl." He releases my nipple, and I cry out from the cold, sharp rush of blood that returns, the sensation like a hot wire extending from my breast to my core.

"And what do I need, baby?" he asks as he turn me around so that I'm facing the hanging clothes. "Why does having you here make me hard? Why does seeing you bound and your ass red from my palm make me want to fuck you until you scream my name?"

"Control," I whisper, and hear his sharp sigh of agreement. "Because even if the world is crashing down around us and it feels like there's nothing you can control, you can still control me. Please," I beg, because his words have taken me that much further. "Please."

He pulls my skirt up, then yanks my panties down around my ankles. I step out of them, and he strokes my rear. I close my eyes, imagining the sting of his palm. Craving it. So much sweeter than the blade, and yet still giving me something to cling to so that I can pull myself out of the mire.

"I will always give you what you need," he says, punctuating the final word with his palm on my ass. I cry out, imagining the red flush on my skin, and then close my eyes as he rubs his palm over the tender flesh. "Whatever and however you need it," he says, then spanks me again, this time sliding his fingers between my legs after the impact, then moaning when he finds me wet and open and ready.

"You like that." It's not a question, and I'm glad he knows

the answer because I'm too gone to answer. I hear his zipper and then the soft swish of material as he sheds his clothes. I expect the press of his cock against me, but instead I feel his fingers tracing my perineum, and making me tremble with anticipation.

He spanks me again and again. Four times, five, until I can't take it anymore. Not the pain—it's shifted into something warm and compelling—but the desperate throbbing. The need to feel him inside me. And I beg for him to please, please fuck me.

"Anything you need," he says, this time with a tease in his voice. He turns me around, and with my wrists still bound, he lifts me so that my legs are around him as he enters me, and he's holding my ass in one hand and keeping me steady with his other palm against my back.

I'm completely open, totally vulnerable, and he's entirely in control. He takes me hard and fast, thrusting so deep inside me I feel as though I'll split in two. And when a violent orgasm rips through me, I tremble in his arms, my core clenching tight around him, drawing him in until he explodes inside me, and then holds me close, suspended in the air even as my senses come back to earth.

When we can move, he has me slide my legs down, then unties the sash. We collapse to the floor and curl up together. "I'm so sorry," he murmurs. "I never meant to pull away. I never meant for there to be distance. I only wanted you to have the chance to heal."

"How could I without you?"

"How could we if not together?" he says, and that is enough apology for me.

When we finally emerge from the closet, Damien takes my hand. "Get dressed," he says. "There's something we need to do."

I'm not sure what he has in mind, but I pull on jeans and a

T-shirt and follow him out to the third-floor sitting area. He looks around the room, finally picking up the pot of daisies that Jamie and Ryan had sent. "Come on," he says, leading me to the stairs.

I follow him outside, and we go to the edge of the house where there's a small flower garden. Someone left a spade on the bench, and since I know the staff well enough to know none of them would leave a tool lying around, I'm certain that Damien put it there earlier.

I look up at him curiously. "What are we—"

"We're planting the flowers," he says. "In her memory."

My eyes burn, but I don't cry. Instead I nod, a little over-whelmed and a lot melancholy. Then I bend to my knees and take the spade he offers me. I dig a hole, and he puts the flowers inside, then pats the earth back down around it.

We sit there for a moment, and I realize I don't know what to say. But Damien speaks first. "Rest in peace, sweet baby," he says, and I nod. *That*, I think, *is enough*.

We sit on the bench and share the bittersweet moment in silence until, finally, I speak. "Mother said it was for the best." I hadn't told him at the time, but now I want him to know. Not only what she said, but that I can deal with her words, now. "She said I could never be a good mother."

His eyes search my face. "Do you believe her?"

"No. I did—or I wanted to. I felt so kicked in the gut." I flash a sharp grin. "I'm feeling stronger now."

"Your mother is a fool, because you would have made an exceptional mother to that child. You know it as well as I do, but you let your mother get in your head. That woman doesn't deserve to walk the same ground you do, much less get inside your mind."

"I know," I say, but I must not sound convincing, because he continues.

"You think the fact that you cut means you'd be a bad

mother? I think the fact that you battled down the temptation—that you constantly prove your strength—is proof that you'll be an excellent parent."

He squeezes my hand as I let his words wash over me, giving me another kind of strength. "She says you're weak? You're not. But even if you were, so what? Strength without weakness is just a number. But you, baby . . . you can point to how far you've come."

"With you beside me," I remind him.

"And *you* beside *me*. You're my strength, Nikki. We both know that. And there's no shame in needing the person you love." His smile touches his eyes. "I actually think that's the point."

I laugh, and taste the salt of my tears as I do.

"I love you," I say. Then I take his hand as we both look down at the freshly planted daisies.

It's time to move on, I think. And with Damien at my side, I know that I can.

25

The next few weeks pass swiftly and easily, solidifying my certainty that even if we aren't fully healed, we're definitely on the path.

Noah's no longer working for me, though he did help me vet the two new employees who took his place, and they're settling in quickly. Eric and Abby, both of whom are not only competent but personable.

I've made two trips back to Dallas, and Damien came with me both times. The meetings went well, and everything for the project is going smoothly—we're even a full week ahead of schedule.

Best of all, there were no ghosts in Dallas.

Now, I sit quietly at my desk before Eric and Abby arrive and go over my notes from last night's conference call with Bijan. I want to organize them quickly so that I can pass them off to Abby to handle, as I've got something else I need to take care of.

I've spent the last week with something other than work sneaking into my thoughts. I've logged hours on the Internet, reading and researching. I know exactly what I want to do.

And I desperately hope that Damien agrees with me.

At a quarter to nine, Abby pops her head into my office, her blond curls bobbing. "Hey, just wanted you to know I'm here. I'm going to dive into debugging that—"

"Hold that thought," I say. "I just emailed you my notes from last night's conference. Can you go through them, prioritize the tasks, and then divide the work between you and Eric?"

"Um, sure." She frowns. "You don't want to do that yourself?"

I laugh, because she's gotten to know me pretty well in a short time. "I'm working on my delegation skills," I say. "Plus, there's somewhere I need to be. You up for it?"

"Absolutely," she says, standing tall. She's young, but ambitious, and now that I've handed her this project, it shows. "Take your time," she says. "Take the day if you need to."

"I might," I say, then grab my purse. "I'll let you know."

I'm smiling as I take the stairs down to the lobby, then out to the parking lot. And that same smile is on my face when I reach the Stark Children's Foundation camp site.

Damien's already there, leaning against a hewn wooden post and answering emails on his phone. He looks up when he sees me, his brow furrowed. "Should I be worried?"

"Worried? Why?"

He cocks his head then starts ticking reasons off on his fingers. "Because you're deep in the thick of the project, you talked to Bijan last night, and you wouldn't leave Abby or Eric in charge this soon without a very good reason."

"All true. I do have a good reason. But there's nothing to worry about." I head toward the path that leads around the main building. "I want to show you something."

We walk together to the back of the building, then climb the stairs that lead up to a second-floor balcony. From there, we have a view of the campsite, and all the kids who are out there. Some playing ball, some swimming. A few riding horses in the distance. Some are just sitting in small groups talking with each other.

All of them look happy.

"You did that, you know," I say.

I see the question on his face when he turns to look at me.

"This place," I explain. "You built it, and it's amazing. Because of you, these kids have life in their faces. They know somebody cares about them."

"Yes," he says, though he sounds a bit confused. "That's the most fundamental goal of the foundation."

"*Your* foundation." I take his hand. "You'll make an incredible father, you know."

I hear his breath hitch. We haven't talked about kids in weeks, though I know we both sit on the bench by the daisies often.

"Don't do this to yourself, baby," he says softly. "Don't do it to me."

I don't answer. I just give him a tug. "Follow me," I order, then lead him through the door that leads from the balcony to the building's second floor. We take the stairs, and then head down the corridor to his office. Inside, I log onto his computer and go to a website that I've been spending a great deal of time exploring.

"There," I say pointing to the screen.

He focuses on it, so long that I start to worry he hates the idea. Then he turns to me, and I see the same hope on his face that I feel in my heart. "Adoption," he says. "You want to adopt a baby from China?"

"A toddler, actually," I say. "And yes. I've been thinking about it for a while." I take his hand. "I want this. I want a family, Damien. I want us to have a family."

Even as I say the words, I can't deny the irony. For so long, I'd wanted to build my business and then worry about children. Now, it's the thought of a family that weighs so heavily on my mind. It's a sad truth that the odds are good I'll never feel a baby growing inside me again. But that doesn't mean I can't be a mom.

He turns to look at the screen again. "They all have some sort of special need," he says, reading the information.

"Yes," I agree. "Most are relatively minor. But all the babies in the system are considered special needs. They call them waiting children. They need our help, just like the kids here."

I stand behind him so that I can see the screen, too, my hands on his shoulders. "I thought first about adopting one of the foundation kids, actually. I mean, so many of them need permanent homes. But I thought it looked too much like singling one of them out, and I didn't want hurt feelings in the rest of them."

"Yes," Damien says, "that makes sense."

I move around beside him and press my hand over his on the desk. "So you're really into the idea?" I'd thought I might have to ease him toward it. Give it time to settle. But he looks ready. Hell, he looks eager.

"I am. To be honest, I've been thinking a bit about adoption lately."

"Really?" The fact that we'd been on the same path makes me feel warm inside. "And it doesn't bother you that the child won't be ours biologically?"

"Are you kidding?" he scoffs. "Blood is biology. It's not family."

My smile blooms so wide it's almost painful. "Let me show you something else," I say, scooting in front of him so that I can sit at the keyboard. "I know this is fast," I say as I move the mouse, clicking on links until I find the image I'm looking for—a little girl of almost a year with a sad face and eyes that captured me the moment I saw her.

"I saw her picture, and she just pulled me in. She needs a family, Damien," I say. "I think she needs us."

I look up at him and see his chin tremble just slightly as he reaches out and presses his fingertips to the computer screen. "Yes," he says softly. "I think she does."

Over the next few days, we go on a series of dinner and cocktails dates with friends so that we can share our news. They're all enthusiastic, but I think Sylvia's squeal is the loudest. I figure that makes sense—after all, she adopted Ronnie right after she married Jackson.

Jamie almost crushed my ribs with the force of her hug, then promised to be the best aunt ever. "Seriously," she'd said. "Best. Aunt. I mean, I'll even sign up for the Learning Annex class if I need to. In case there are rules and shit." And Ryan slapped Damien on the back in a manly sort of way, and then said they needed to go have a celebratory cigar on the back patio.

Evelyn got choked up, but managed to hold it together. Sofia clapped like a little girl and started to throw her arms around Damien in a hug. She stopped herself, then looked at me, and only finished the embrace after I'd given her a nod.

Frank was the one who truly surprised me. I actually saw tears in his eyes, and when he hugged me and said he was proud of me, I started to cry myself.

But those are the people I knew would support us. I'm meeting my mother in an hour, and I really don't expect the same kind of warm reception.

"You don't have to tell her anything," Damien says. We're in the Tower apartment, and I'm pacing in front of the wall of windows that overlooks the city.

"I do," I say, though I can't explain why I'm so insistent. Maybe I'm hoping to give her one last chance. Maybe I'm kicking my own ass, pushing the issue so I'll have the impetus to finally and truly cut the strings.

Either way, I'm about to head downstairs to the plaza. I've told her I want to meet her for coffee at the Java B's outside.

"Do you want me to come?" he asks.

"Want, yes. But I think I need to do this alone. If I need you, you're only fifty-seven stories away."

He bends to kiss me. "I'm never that far away."

I nod, then cling to him for a moment. "Wish me luck."

"Luck," he says, walking me to the elevator. The car is already there, but he takes my arm to hold me back before I step on. "I poked around a bit," he says. "Your mom's house in Dallas was going into foreclosure."

"What?"

"She's broke," he says. "I don't know why she really came to Los Angeles, but I have a feeling she thinks there's a payday at the end of the line somehow."

I nod, not surprised, but still a little numb.

"I wanted you to know before you talked to her."

"Okay. Thanks." I lift myself up on my toes to kiss him. "I guess we'll find out," I say, and then step into the car. Soon enough, I'm off the elevator and across the lobby to the plaza. She's already there, standing with perfect posture by the fountain.

"They have tables over there," I say. "Grab a seat and I'll get us both a latte."

She does, and I use the few moments while I'm ordering and waiting for the drinks to get my act together. Then I join her at the table and decide to cut straight to the chase. "I wanted to meet you so that I could give you my news. Damien and I have decided to adopt."

"Have you?" Her brows lift almost imperceptibly.

"From China," I continue. "We've submitted the initial paperwork for a little girl. We're meeting with the agency tomorrow, and then we start the home study process. And the wait."

"Home study," she says. "Where a stranger comes in to evaluate you?"

I put on a cheery smile. "Yup. Pretty much."

"Hmm," she says, then sips her coffee. "And you're adopting from China? My friend Angelica's daughter just adopted from China. She was infertile, too." Her voice is like fingernails on a chalkboard. "I understand all the children have something wrong with them."

A knot of anger forms in my stomach, and I tell myself to just ignore it. "I wouldn't put it that way, but all the children in the program do have special needs."

"And this child you're interested in? What's the matter with her?"

I mentally bang my head on the table. "She has an extra toe on each foot. It's really no big deal. We've already spoken with a surgeon about what's involved to correct it."

"I see," she says, though I sincerely doubt she does.

"Well," I say. "That's really all I wanted to tell you. I'm sure you have a busy day and all that . . ."

She makes no move to leave. "I can't say that I ever considered adoption, but I do think that a woman should want children so long as she can keep her figure and her husband happy." She looks appraisingly at me. "At least this way you don't have to worry about baby weight. But do you think Damien will be happy with a child who's not his own blood?"

"I know he will be."

Her mouth pinches together, and she inhales loudly through her nose. "You're blind, Nichole. You always have been where that man is concerned. Do you really think a man like Damien Stark wants a child who isn't his flesh and blood? He won't. I've seen it before, you know. You can't hold a man like that without the tie of blood."

"What are you talking about?"

"My father—your grandfather—he was my mother's second husband and my stepfather. Do you think he cared a whit about me? I was never enough. Never polished enough or pretty

enough. I was an irritation until I grew up, and then I was simply his heir by virtue of the fact that he had no other."

I've never heard my mother talk about my grandfather that
way. "I didn't know that," I say. "But that's not what Damien's
like."

"So you say now. Men don't stay. Your sister learned that the
hard way. I don't want you to suffer the same. But you will.
He'll leave you. You give that man a child that's not his blood
and he'll walk away."

"No, he won't." I lean back. "The thing is, I've been thinking
a lot about families. Family isn't about blood. Blood is an accident. Blood is biology. Family is love and respect and caring
and commitment."

"Commitment! Is that why he's been tooling around with
that crazy bitch from London?"

"Sofia?" I tilt my head, examining her face. "What do you
know about Sofia?"

Her eyes dart away, and I have the impression that she's
kicking herself for saying too much. "I saw it online," she says
vaguely.

"Since when have you hung out on social media? Christ,
Mother," I say, pushing my chair back to stand. "You're the one
who sent that email?"

"I don't know what you're talking about. But if you're suggesting that someone told you about your husband and that
trollop, then I think you should thank them."

"Go," I say.

"What?"

"You heard me. I want you to go. We're done."

"But what . . . I don't . . ."

"You understand me just fine," I say. "And it's time for you
to leave."

"Fine." She pushes back her chair and stands up. "You
always were an impossible child." She hitches her purse up on

her shoulder. "Do you really think they'll allow you to adopt? With your . . . issues?"

There's something cold in her tone. Something that makes me reach for the back of my chair to steady myself. "You mean the fact that I used to cut?"

"I would think an agency would be very disturbed by that fact. If they were to find out. If they were to see photos. Hear the stories. And of course, it would be terribly embarrassing if your history went public."

"Are you *threatening* me?"

She sits back down. "I'm concerned about your welfare. I don't want you taking on more than you can handle. And, of course, I'm looking out for the best interest of the child."

Fury pounds in my ears, and I grip the back of the chair so hard I'm afraid I'm going to break it. But then I take a breath, because the bigger picture is coming into focus. Because this isn't about me or Damien or my child. Where my mother is concerned, it never is.

This is about her. And I know exactly what to do.

"You know what, Mother? You win."

"Excuse me?"

"You win. You're going to go back to Texas. To your new, mortgage-free house and your lovely new Mercedes and a six-figure bank account."

"What on earth—"

"Don't act surprised. It's what you want. And it's yours. If you go in the morning. And if you stay the hell out of my affairs."

"You think you're so special because you have money now? That you're going to take pity on your poor mother who lost her fortune. It wasn't my fault, you know. And that money isn't yours at all."

"Take it or leave it, Mother. But decide now."

This was her end game all along. Cash. And I'm more than

happy to have realized it now. Because I want this over. I want her gone.

"Be at the airport in the morning," I order. "You remember where we keep the jet hangared? If you're not there, the deal's off."

"I will," Mother says. "But only because your perception is so skewed. I know this isn't forever, no matter what you say. You're just like your sister, and eventually you'll come crawling back to me. You've never stood on your own. And when he leaves, we both know that you're going to be destroyed."

"He won't," I say. "I know it. And you know what, Mother? You know it, too. Maybe Ashley wasn't strong. But I am." I move around the table to stand closer to her. "But we don't need to argue about it. You win, remember?"

I start to walk away, then pause and look back at her. "Actually, I guess we both win. Because you'll finally be gone. Goodbye, Mother. We're done."

And then I turn my back on her and, with my heart pounding wildly, I walk back into Stark Tower and take the elevator up to Damien.

26

"You're sure you don't mind?" We're in bed, and I'm propped up beside him, my fingertip tracing patterns on his chest as I run down the drama with my mother.

"Paying to get her out of our hair? I think it's money well spent."

I sigh, relieved. "Good. I know I should have asked first, but—"

"It's your money, too," he reminds me, which is a little fact I never seem to remember.

"Do you think she'll tell the agency anyway? About my cutting, I mean? Once she has the deed to the house, there's not much we can do. At least not easily. And she could tell them anonymously, so we couldn't even prove it as her."

"She might," Damien says. "I wouldn't put it past her."

I close my eyes, then blow out a breath. "It won't matter if she does. I'm going to tell them myself."

He shifts, then tilts my chin up so that I'm looking straight at him. "Are you sure?"

I nod. "Better to be upfront. Besides, I want to do this right. They do an evaluation. They talk to the family beforehand.

I don't want to have to dodge questions. I want to just be me. The real me, with no mask at all."

"No child could ask for a better mother."

I quirk a brow as I look at him. "Hopefully, the agency and China will agree with you."

I push myself up to sitting, my mind still going over the conversation with my mother.

"What is it?" Damien asks.

"It's just . . . well, she said I can't stand on my own. That if you leave, it would destroy me." I swallow, then look at him. "She's right, you know. I love you so damn much."

He shakes his head. "Love isn't reliance, baby." He strokes my hair, his eyes looking deep into mine. "The truth is, you can stand on your own. But you choose to stand with me."

"Yes." The word is almost a gasp, and I cling to him as relief and understanding floods through me. "Yes," I repeat. "I choose you."

"And that makes me a very lucky man."

"Damien?"

"Yes?"

"Would you make love to me now?"

I feel the vibrations of his low chuckle in his chest. "Baby," he says, rolling over and trapping me beneath him, "it would be my pleasure."

Slowly, he peels off the T-shirt I'm wearing, leaving me naked beneath him. He does the same with his sweatpants, tossing them in a heap on the floor. He kisses me sweetly, his hands caressing me, gentle strokes. Sensual movements.

There is nothing wild about the way we make love tonight, and yet it is no less passionate than when he takes me hard and fast, claiming me with such fervor it leaves me breathless.

Tonight, it's tender kisses that take my breath away. And when he spreads my legs and slides inside me, our eyes stay locked and he thrusts inside me, my hips rising in a matching rhythm that draws him in deeper and deeper, until we feel like one person, the boundaries between where I end and he begins merging together.

"Yes," I murmur when I'm so close I can feel the climax pounding against me. "Oh, Damien, yes."

He thrusts harder, his mouth closing over mine. I cling to his back, my hands sliding down to cup his ass, wanting to feel him deeper, and deeper still. And then, suddenly, the tempo of his thrusts increase, and his weight is pushing me into the mattress, and I feel the tension inside me growing and growing, until finally Damien growls in my ear for me to come with him—to explode with him.

And as if his voice is a command, I shatter under the force of his will, a billion points of light bursting from me, as pleasure rips me apart completely.

I can only tremble and breathe and cling to Damien until the orgasm fades. Then he pulls me close and I mold my body against his.

"I love you, baby," he says.

"I love you, too." My voice is thin, my eyelids heavy. And the last thing I think as sleep draws me under is that tomorrow, everything will change.

And I really can't wait.

I flash a nervous smile at Damien as we approach the door of the adoption agency. His left hand is twined with my right, and in my left I hold the photo I'd printed off the Internet of the little girl we've begun to call Lara. The child I hope will soon be our daughter.

"You're sure?" Damien asks. "If you tell them everything, they may say no. Not let us adopt. And it all may come out— you and I both know there are no secrets that are safe."

I nod, knowing that he's right. If I don't tell and they find out, we'll be denied for sure. If I do tell, I'll end up in a room with a psychologist who will decide if I'm fit to adopt. I'll have to pour out my heart, my history. I'll have to open up in a way I haven't opened up to anyone but Damien. And it will be painful and horrible and embarrassing.

It will also be worth it.

"They won't deny us," I say. "Maybe I am a cutter. Maybe I always will be. But I'm a cutter who got it under control. Who doesn't need the blade anymore. Because of you," I add, and he squeezes my hand.

I draw in a breath. "More important, I'll be a damn good mom."

"You will," he says. "You absolutely will."

"And if they deny us, we'll try another country or another agency or private adoption. Or we'll have a baby ourselves. The odds aren't entirely against us," I add, though the thought of multiple miscarriages before we finally hit that magical statistic makes me want to cry right then.

"I don't want you to go through that again," he says, following my thoughts.

"I would, though. Because I want this. I'm certain of it. More certain than I've been about anything," I add, looking at him. "Except you."

"I love you," he says.

And then he opens the door, and we step through it into our future.

Epilogue

I laugh as I step into the jet's doorway and see the *Welcome Home* sign held up between Jamie and Ryan on the tarmac below. I descend the ramp, our twenty-month-old daughter clinging to me like a little monkey, and Damien following closely behind.

"I think everyone we've ever met is here," I say, looking around at the crowd of friends and family gathered in front of one of the Stark hangars at the Santa Monica Airport. Jamie and Ryan, Sylvia and Jackson and their kids, Evelyn and my dad. Ollie's here, too, as is Sofia, along with Dallas and Jane, Cass and Siobhan, Lyle and Noah and Wyatt. Rachel and Edward and at least two dozen other people from Stark International, as well.

"There's more of a crowd inside," Jamie says. "Be forewarned. We had to give our girl a proper homecoming, didn't we?" she asks as she waves at the baby. "Say hi to your Aunt Jamie," she says, and my brilliant daughter lifts her hand in reply and giggles.

"Everyone," Damien says, his voice happy and strong. "Thank you all for coming. It means a lot to all three of us. And speaking of three, I'd like to formally introduce you to Lara Ashley Stark. Come here, you," he says, holding out his hands for me to pass Lara to him.

"*Baba*," she squeals, using the Mandarin word for Daddy. "Kiss!"

Everyone claps, and she ducks her head shyly against Damien's chest.

"That was the first word we taught her," I say proudly. "And it's become her favorite." I stroke her hair. "Hasn't it, sweetie? Kiss?"

"Kiss!" she says again, then laughs and laughs. "*Baba*! Kiss!"

"Anything for my girl," Damien says, then rubs his nose against hers, buzzes her cheeks with his eyelashes, then gives her a kiss.

"Kiss," I say, laughing, and he pulls me close and gives me a kiss of my own as our friends applaud, and a warm, comfortable glow washes over me.

It's been more than eight months since we started the process, and I can't believe that we've finally reached the end—or, really, the beginning. It's a whole new chapter in our life together, and I take Damien's hand as our little family follows the crowd into the hangar.

"Don't worry," Syl says, sliding in beside me. "We know you're exhausted. This will be a short party. We just couldn't wait."

"It's fine," I tell her, happy to show Lara off, especially since she's warmed to the crowd and is smiling and giggling, safe in Damien's arms. "I'm not that tired, anyway," I admit. That's one of the perks of traveling in your own jet. An actual bed in an actual bedroom—and on this trip, even a crib for the baby.

Damien takes her through the crowd in the hangar, and though she mostly clings to him, a few of our friends get anointed with Lara's affection, including Evelyn, who takes her with gusto, lifting her high and making the kind of silly faces I never thought I'd see on my friend. And when Frank leans down and starts making animal noises for her, I have to turn away so that I don't completely lose it.

Ronnie wants to hold her, but we settle for putting her on a blanket and letting Ronnie and Jeffery babysit their cousin until their attention wears out.

As for the party, it goes on longer than anyone intended, but I can hardly complain, especially since our princess is having such a good time.

"Up!" she demands to Cass at one point, and when Cass complies, she points to the diamond stud in Cass's nose and says something that I assume means "shiny."

"She's wonderful," Ollie says, coming to sit by me as Cass brings her over and puts her on a blanket spread out in front of the sofa I've claimed. "Just like her mother," he adds.

"She's smart and fearless," I counter. "Just like her dad."

He chuckles. "That, too," he says, then puts an arm around me as we both look down at my daughter. "I'm glad I was in town tonight. You did good. You and Damien."

I smile and watch the room, then smile even broader when Damien comes to sit across from us, pausing to shake Ollie's hand before he drops, exhausted, into his chair.

Sofia comes up with a smile for Damien, but it's me she looks at when she asks, "May I hold her?"

I hesitate.

"I'll give her back," Sofia says blandly.

"Crap," I say. "I'm sorry. Of course, you can. I—"

She laughs. "It's okay. Really. And I'm going back to London tomorrow. But I had to be here for this, so I flew in this morning."

She bends down and scoops up Lara, who doesn't fuss, even though her eyes are starting to droop. "I wanted to meet her and see Damien in the role of daddy. I figure he'll do better than all his role models," she says, with a wry look in his direction.

"I damn well better," he says, raising a bottle of water in a mock toast.

"Do you want to stay longer?" I ask her. "It's okay," I add, meeting Damien's eyes. I'm still not one-hundred percent on the Sofia-train, but I also know I won't get there without spending more time together. And I know it's important to Damien that Sofia be a part of Lara's life.

She hesitates, her eyes glistening as she flashes a watery smile. "No. But thank you. I have sessions scheduled with the headshrinker—I don't want to miss them." She kisses Lara's head. "I'll be back, though. We'll ease into it slowly, okay?"

"Yeah," I say, meaning it. "That's totally okay."

Sofia puts the baby back down, and then she and Ollie both step away to mingle some more.

As soon as Ollie leaves, Damien moves to sit beside me. "Well, I'm exhausted," he says as he reaches down to pick up Lara. "Come here, little girl. You wore your daddy out."

He leans back in the seat, Lara pressed against his chest, sucking her thumb.

"You can't possibly be tired, Mr. Stark," I tease.

"Believe me, I can."

"Mmm. Well, that presents a problem."

"Oh, really?" I see the fire ignite in his eyes. "Do you have something energetic to suggest when we get home?"

"Always," I say with a grin. "But I was thinking more in terms of the children. I mean if one wears you out, how are you going to manage two?"

Very slowly, he turns to me. "Say that again."

I take his hand, and gently press his palm over the secret I've been keeping. "Doctor Tyler says I'm out of the danger zone. I—I didn't want to say anything until, well, until we were sure everything is okay."

"And you're sure now?" The hope in his voice is almost palpable.

I nod. "I saw him right before we left for China. My statistical chance of something going wrong now is the same as any other woman."

"But we weren't trying."

"We weren't trying the first time, either," I remind him. "I'm a walking billboard for failed birth control."

"You're pregnant," he says slowly, a tender awe lighting his face. "You're really pregnant."

I laugh, delighted by his reaction. "Lara's going to be a big sister," I say, unable to stop smiling.

He pulls me close, his eyes dancing. "Kiss!" Lara orders. "Kiss!"

"You know what?" Damien says. "I think I will."

And with our little girl between us, he kisses me long and hard.

"Is it a boy or a girl?" he asks, when he gently pulls away.

"One or the other," I say, snuggling against him as I fight a smile. "Either way, it's wonderful."

Author's Note

If you're reading this note before reading the book, be aware that there are spoilers below!

This is a book that is near and dear to my heart. Not only because I'm happy to finally give readers what you've been asking for—a family for Nikki and Damien—but because the story itself is personal. Not true, but personal.

In late October of 2006, my husband and oldest daughter (who turned five during the trip) traveled to China to adopt our youngest child, a sweet little girl born with a cleft lip and palate. She turned three during the adoption trip . . . and as of this writing, she's thirteen. And she and her sister are the light of our lives (and also pretty typical teens!).

Like Nikki and Damien, my husband and I saw her picture on an adoption agency website, and we immediately knew that she was our daughter. That one glimpse began a lifelong journey filled with laughter and love.

While China's adoption program has changed over the years, what hasn't changed is that many "special needs" kids are still needing homes and help. Often, the need is very minor. If you're interested in adopting, I encourage you to contact one of the many agencies that specialize in international adoptions. And if you just want to help, please consider donating to one of the many organizations that help orphans in China. Two I have personal familiarity with are Love Without Boundaries (which provides medical care, including cleft lip and palate repair for Chinese orphans) and Half the Sky (which provides educational services, including services at orphanages such as the one my daughter lived in).

Thank you, and happy reading!

XXOO
JK

It began with an unforgettable indecent
proposal from Damien Stark...

...But only his passion could set
Nikki Fairchild free.

The irresistible, erotic, emotionally charged
Stark series.

Available now from

A wedding, a honeymoon, a Valentine's Day,
a trip to Vegas and a Christmas
Damien Stark-style means one thing...

Happy Ever After is just the beginning...

The steamily seductive, dazzlingly romantic
Stark Ever After Novellas.

Available now from

Sylvia Brooks never lets anyone get too close.

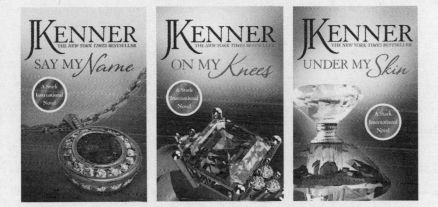

But Jackson Steele is the only man who's ever made her feel alive.

Return to the smoking hot Stark world with the explosive Stark International trilogy.

Available now from

It was wrong for Dallas Sykes and
Jane Martin to be together...

But it was even harder for
them to be apart...

Three gorgeous, enigmatic and
powerful men…

…and the striking women who can bring
them to their knees.

Enthralling and sizzling hot, the Most Wanted series.

Available now from

HEADLINE
ETERNAL

FIND YOUR HEART'S DESIRE...

VISIT OUR WEBSITE: www.headlineeternal.com
FIND US ON FACEBOOK: facebook.com/eternalromance
FOLLOW US ON TWITTER: @eternal_books
EMAIL US: eternalromance@headline.co.uk